CASS LIBRARY OF AFRICAN STUDIES

AFRICANA MODERN LIBRARY

No. 12

General Editor: Professor E. U. Essien-Udom
University of Ibadan, Nigeria

LETTERS

ON THE

POLITICAL CONDITION OF
THE GOLD COAST

Since the Exchange of Territory Between
The English and Dutch Governments, on January 1, 1868

together with a Short Account of

The Ashantee War, 1862-4, and the Awoonah War, 1866

. BY .

AFRICANUS B. HORTON

SECOND EDITION

With a New Introduction by
E. A. AYANDELE
Department of History, University of Ibadan

FRANK CASS & CO. LTD.
1970

Published by
FRANK CASS AND COMPANY LIMITED
67 Great Russell Street, London WC1

New introduction Copyright © 1970 A. E. Ayandele

| First edition | 1870 |
| Second edition | 1970 |

SBN 7146 1758 X

Printed in Great Britain by Clarke, Doble & Brendon Ltd.
Plymouth and London

INTRODUCTION TO THE
SECOND EDITION

James Africanus Beale Horton lived for forty-eight years only — 1835 to 1883. But although he died at a rather tender age his life was noble, renowned and rich, in many ways a veritable inspiration to the first and second generation African educated elite in West Africa in the second half of the nineteenth century. In the academic realm he was a pride to Africa because his intellectual talent flourished to a degree which won official commendation at King's College, London, in 1858; that invested his publications with an excellence, maturity and scholarship recognised by contemporary European critics; that made his *Physical and Medical Climate and Meteorology of the West Coast of Africa* (London, 1867) the first scientific work on Africa written and published by a West African. In the European medical profession he shared with the more elderly W. B. Davies the honour of being the only Africans in the nineteenth century to serve in the medical department of the British Army in West Africa, a position which both filled with such credit that they attained the status of Surgeon-Major (Lieutenant Colonel rank). In the history of literary education Horton is remembered as being the first African to advocate that the Fourah Bay Institution should become the earliest university institution of West Africa, whilst in banking his name must go down as founder of the first bank in the territory.

By his father, Beale Horton belonged to the Ibo ethnic group of Nigeria. Rescued on the high seas by the British anti-slave West African Squadron, James Horton — as his father came to be called — was settled at Gloucester, a small village in the mountain district, only a few miles from Freetown, the premier settlement of the Sierra Leone Colony which had been founded in 1787 by British philanthropists. It is not known whether Beale's parents were among the 107 newly-rescued America-bound slaves with whom the Reverend Henry During, of the Church Missionary Society, founded Gloucester on 18 December, 1816. However it is clear that his father was among the first generation of carpenters of the village and that both parents renounced traditional religion for the Christian faith in which they acquired the reputation of being "pious."[1]

The environment into which Beale Horton was born, which moulded his early life and left some permanent effect upon him, can be gleaned from eye-witness accounts. Although Gloucester became a predominantly Christian settlement in the first five years of its existence — boasting in 1821 that 500 out of a total population of 720 were able to read their Testaments — a decline in its allegiance to Christianity had set in by 1827. Attendance at St. Andrew's church, which had a capacity of 1,500 souls, had shrunk to 145 by this year, the majority of former Christian adherents lapsing into "their former evil habits and country fashions."[2]

The faithful minority — one out of three of the total population of just over a thousand being Church-goers between 1835 and 1842 — constituted themselves into an exclusive group. In reaction to the increasing worldliness of society and convivial gratifications of the lapsing Christians the faithful proclaimed themselves the "righteous" who should have nothing to do whatsoever, including the exchange of greetings, with the "non-righteous".[3] Neither Gloucester nor the puritanical severity of its Christian minority disappeared completely from Horton's mind. Thus in 1865 when he urged the British to establish an industrial institute in West Africa for the training of carpenters, shoe-makers, masons and wheel-rights, it was his birth-

1. C.M.S. (London) CAI/0129 E. Jones, "Report of the Christian Institutions" 10/4/1855.
2. C.M.S. CAI/080 Thomas Davey, "Report of the Mountain Districts" 19/12/1827.
3. C.M.S. CAI/042 W. K. Betts *Journals*, 25/3/1832.

place, a village less ideally-situated than neighbouring Regent and other locations in West Africa, which he suggested as the ideal site.[4] In life, too, be became an apostle of total abstinence in matters of alcohol, becoming patron of the Advanced Guard Lodge of the Independent Order of Good Templars of the Gold Coast.[5]

Although he was their seventh and only surviving child out of eight, Beale Horton's parents were so poor that they could not afford a literary education for their son at any level. Consequently from infancy to the university Horton was nurtured by British philanthropists. At the primary level his mentor and guardian was a C.M.S. missionary, the Reverend James Beale, whose names were adopted wholesale by Horton in his early years in appreciation of the missionary's foster-paternity. In the third quarter of 1847, on the recommendation of this missionary, but at the expense of the African Native Agency Committee, young Horton was admitted "on trial" to the C.M.S. Grammar School, Freetown;[6] this secondary grammar school, the first in West Africa, which was to turn out about 970 students within twenty-five years, had been founded in March 1845 to gratify the secular aspirations of the Sierra Leone community. In this institution Horton had the opportunity of reading Greek, Latin, Astronomy, Mathematics, Natural Philosophy, Music and English History and of learning cotton growing.

On 3 January 1853, in the hope of training for a career in the Church, he entered the Fourah Bay Institution. It was here that his latent gift for book- learning began to be recognised. In character he was observed by his Principal as being "somewhat mercurial in temper" and lacking in humility; but in his studies he was "a quick and promising young man" who had "the *root of the matter* in him."[7] When therefore in 1855 the C.M.S. were requested by the

---

4. *African Times* (London) 23/10/1866.
5. *West African Reporter* (Sierra Leone) 21/5/1879.
6. C.M.S. CAI/0173 T. Peyton *Journals*, 25/9/1847
7. C.M.S. CAI/0129 E. Jones "Report of the Christian Institutions" 10/4/1855

War Office to recommend three African youths for a medical career in the British Army in West Africa, the lot fell on Horton, although he had one year more to complete at Fourah Bay and was younger than the two others — Samuel Campbell and W. B. Davies — who had completed their studies at the same institution.

The year he lost at Fourah Bay did not affect his performance in his medical studies in London and Edinburgh. It is worthy of remark that, unlike their English colleagues, their lack of previous knowledge of anatomy, physiology, chemistry and natural history notwithstanding, Horton and Davies held their own in these subjects.[8] By 1858 they had qualified as medical doctors, Horton acquitting himself with distinction in his class. In the language of Dr. R. N. Jelf, the Principal of King's College, who spoke of his excellent conduct and diligence *"in the warmest terms"*, Horton "gained the prize in surgery and five certificates of Honour in different branches of Medical Instruction. At the end of his cause (sic.) he was on the recommendation of myself and the professors elected by the Council to the Associateship of the College, a distinction which always implies not only proficiency in studies but also an unimpeachable academical character."[9] A year in Edinburgh earned Horton and Davies the M.D. In one year alone, the former was able to produce a publishable doctorate dissertation, *The Medical Topography of the West Coast of Africa, with Sketches of its Botany*, which had already gone to press when he sailed for West Africa in September, 1859.

The two Africans, who had been appointed as Staff Assistant Surgeons on 5 September 1859, had hoped that they would serve in the Army Medical Department of Sierra Leone but, in spite of petition by the community there for their retention, if only for a month, they were ordered to proceed to the Gold Coast within thirty-six hours. On 18 October they arrived in the country where

8. Samuel Campbell dropped out as a result of illness.
9. C.M.S. CAI/0117 Testimonial dated 3/11/1858.

they were to sojourn for the greater part of their career; Horton being sent almost immediately to Anamaboe and Davies to Dixcove.

The promoters of the opportunity enjoyed by the African surgeons – the War Office and the C.M.S. – had been prompted by two motives. The former had been primarily concerned about the fatality of West Africa to the white medical personnel. It was believed that Africans were likely to survive in their fatherland better than the Europeans, that they would possess immunity to yellow fever, dysentry, heat and humidity that appeared to be harmful to the white man's health. In this sense the training of Horton and Davies was an experiment which, if successful, should have marked the beginning of the mass training of Africans in medicine for service on the coast. But for Henry Venn, the C.M.S. Secretary, the great lover of Africans and dreamer of a literate, sophisticated, Christianised and industrialised West Africa under the control of the educated elite, the training of these two Staff Assistant Surgeons was no more than a part of the fulfilment of his vision.

In the nineteenth century both in popular imagination and, to a great extent in fact, the climate of West Africa, more than any other climate threatened the white man with death. The bill of European mortality was very heavy: one out of every three Europeans in the territory in the pre-Scramble era was buried there. In the Army Medical Department alone, for instance, fifteen out of forty-two Europeans who were employed between 1860 and 1870 succumbed to the climate.[10] During epidemics the toll was heavier. In 1859 yellow fever removed the lives of three medical men at Macarthy's Island in the River Gambia; in Freetown it carried off 160 Europeans, including the Roman Catholic Bishop and four priests who died in the same house. The cholera which smote the Gambia ten years later nearly effaced the European population, taking four-

10. A. A. Gore, *Medical History of Our West African Campaigns.* London 1876 p. 217

teen lives in the month of May alone. The small-pox which
raged on the Gold Coast in 1872 struck terror into the
European inhabitants and earned Horton the warm thanks
of Earl Kimberley and £50 for the zeal and courage with
which he defied the epidemic.[11]

Not a few of the European sojourners in West Africa
returned post-haste to their countries cursing the climate of
the territory for its hostility to their health. Even those
who remained behind lived in perpetual fear which compelled them to observe habits that might seem amusing to
medical scientists today. The habits prescribed were
numerous indeed. For instance Horton advised European
sojourners in West Africa to avoid too much animal food
and too much fruit, unless eaten with a small quantity of
bread or biscuit; the observance of from five to six hour
intervals between meals; "a cup of tea or coffee or even a
glass of cold water with a little bread or biscuit should be
taken before going out in the morning."[12]

Neither the desire of the War Office nor the hope of
Henry Venn for increased African personnel in the Army
Medical Department was to be fulfilled in the nineteenth
century. Both the head of the department and the Commander of Troops in West Africa did not share the ration-
ality and pro-African programme of White Hall and
Salisbury Square respectively. Climatic considerations were
for them of less importance than their conviction, that
Africans should never hold positions which, in their
opinion, should be for whites only.

It should be stressed that although in British West Africa
it was in practically all departments of the civil service that
the white sought to retain a monopoly of the higher posts,
it was in the Medical Department that racial tension was
most acute. This was because several African families were
rich enough to train their children in medicine in British
universities. On their return they were employed by the
Government. Naturally continuous and long service made

11. *West African Reporter* 15/1/1881
12. C.M.S. CAI/0117 J. A. B. Horton, "Health Precautions in West Africa."

these Africans more qualified than the ever-changing and often younger, less experienced and less qualified European colleagues who were invariably employed as their superiors. In the circumstances Africans contended that merit and experience, rather than colour, should determine seniority in the Department.[13]

The Army and Judiciary created little or no tension: no opportunity existed for Africans to aspire to or qualify for the highest posts in these departments. Throughout the nineteenth century, wealth could not secure training for Africans in the army; at best wealth produced a band of legal practitioners. No African was appointed as a Magistrate; no African was trained as a military commander. Following a mutiny, the attempt made in 1851 to raise up an African army — the Gold Coast Artillery Corps — for the purpose of garrisoning British forts was terminated in 1863. The troops were replaced by the 4th West India Regiment.

In these circumstances the monopolist attitude assumed by the controllers of the British Army in West Africa cannot be regarded as surprising. The training of Horton and Davies was viewed by them as an irritating novelty. Until 1859, the threat of the climate notwithstanding, the Army Medical Department had never been in dearth of white applicants. Between 1841 and 1858 not less than 58 people were appointed; between 1860 and 1870 there were no less than 42 recruits.[14] Rather than being deterred by the climate European personnel learned to know its dangers and characteristics, thereby putting themselves in a position to adopt special effective precautions. In the Army, the Judiciary and even in other departments, several officials volunteered to serve terms in the territory.[15] In the Army Medical Department, for instance, Sir Charles Callaghan, Principal Medical Officer who was to condemn the Horton-

13. (Rhodes House, Oxford) Aborigines Protection Society Papers G. 247
   O. Sapara, "Colonial Medical Appointments in West African Colonies."
14. A. A. Gore. Op. cit. pp. 211-212.
15. *African Times.* 23/12/1863.

Davies experiment, was in the early sixties serving for a second time. And it should be added that the white personnel in the Army Medical Department were encouraged to stay on by the privileges offered to them from 1859, privileges not offered in the West Indies, for example. Among these privileges were permission to practice privately, the reckoning of every year's service as two years and the augmentation of their salaries through other jobs conceded to them.

For the directors of the British Army in West Africa, Horton and Davies had passed through the Needle's Eye when they entered the preserve of the white man. The commander of the eighteen-soldier strong army of Anamaboe, the small port to which Horton was posted, administered to him one humiliation after another from the moment he had reported there. According to Horton not only did the commander, one Captain de Ruvignes, receive him with "loathesome coldness" but he also "tormented, disturbed and vexed" the African Staff Assistant Surgeon for "full three months." Apart from threatening "everyday" to whip Horton, he provokingly deprived him of the amenities attached to the post of Assistant Staff Surgeon and sought to incite the rank and file of the army against the African officer. The captain denied Horton cooking facilities, would not allow the African officer's cook — whom he put in ropes,— to prepare food for him, refused to salute or answer greetings and forced Horton "like a schoolboy" to eat with his friends outside the fort.[16]

Horton bore his trials with a great deal of patience, refusing to be provoked or to assert his rights. He made no report to the officer commanding the troops at Cape Coast. Only when the Governor visited Anamaboe in February 1860 did Horton reveal his sufferings. Rather than resort to the British press or return canon for canon in the manner of an Edward Blyden or a James Johnson, he obeyed the peremptory order of the Governor to destroy the day-to-

16. C.M.S. CAI/0117 J. A. Horton to Henry Venn 3/2/1860.

day records of his sufferings and proceed to Quittah, another fort, as the only way to end his bitter experience.[17]

It is puzzling that the mercurial temper noticed in the African Staff Assistant Surgeon at Fourah Bay had subsided and that he was lacking entirely in aggressiveness. As his literary pugilism with negrophobe psuedo-anthropologists of the Anthropological Society of London in subsequent years was to show, he could be combative. As he boasted in 1868: "I will never permit any unjust abuse, any unfounded diatribe against the African race, to be ruthlessly lavished on them without repelling or exposing the calumny."[18] At Anamaboe in 1859 – 60 Horton's patience was a studied one; his appearance of a dumb-driven sheep, a pretended and calculating one. His attitude was based on a great sense of responsibility to the interests of the Negro Race. Like Samuel Ajayi Crowther, the first African Anglican Bishop, Horton was aware that he was an experimental military medical officer, that no excuse or pretext must be given to people like Captain de Ruvignes to discredit highly placed educated Africans as unworthy beneficiaries of British philanthropy on the platform of incapacity to practice virtues. At Anamaboe Horton believed that he should demonstrate the African's extraordinary capacity for patience:

> It is a matter of paramount necessity that as I am amongst the first of the native Africans who have been educated by H. M. Government in the medical profession and sent out in the army as staff assist. (sic) surgeon to practise that noble art amongst my own countrymen and those of the Europeans who may require an attendance, that I should not be too hasty in whatever I am about to undertake — not to give in to the dictate of passion, or take rash measures which the nature of the trials that I am suffering merited. I felt that it was the keystone of the continuance of that whole plan of educating young Africans and sending them in the coast. Should I give way thousands of them here who are hostile to the plan will have grounds to complain.[19]

17. Ibid.
18. J.A.B. Horton, *West African Countries and Peoples*, London 1868, p. IV
19. C.M.S. CAI/0117 J. A. Horton to Henry Venn 3/2/1860.

The belief that the credit of the Negro Race was involved in his career and character had not just come upon him. In Britain he had added the significant emotive and self-advertising word "Africanus" to his name; he had prefaced his M. D. thesis with the hope "that this Publication may be the means of exciting some interest. . . on behalf of Africa."[20] He had also become optimistic about the future progress of Africa, looking forward to inter-tribal marriages in West Africa to "produce the finest race in Africa." Throughout his life he was modestly proud of his record at King's College, London, and Edinburgh University.

Never in his career was Horton to come under another Ruvignes. He came to earn the respect of several European residents and British officials in West Africa as an able doctor; his skill attracted clients from all over the Gold Coast. Among his clients were Governors such as Richard Pine, and European merchants like Henry Barnes. As a European trader, Charles Filason, confided to Horton: "I would sooner be under your medical care than a great many of the youthful Assistant Surgeons I have seen on the coast."[21] In the Army his skill and attributes as a physician were commended by Captains Hole, Herrich and Gabb.

In view of the pleasanter relations he had with other Europeans on the coast, relations enriched by his urbane and suave disposition, Horton did not generalise about the white man or British policy in West Africa from particular incidents or examples. He classified Europeans, in terms of their attitude to Africa and Africans, into two schools of thought, namely the patrons and the enemies of the development of the continent and its peoples. Among the patrons of the true interests of Africa, according to his observation, were the British Government and British missionary and philanthropic agencies like the Church

20. George Shepperson, "An Early African Graduate" *University of Edinburgh Gazette.* p. 24, quotes Horton's thesis.
21. C.M.S. CAI/0117 Charles Filason to Horton 29/10/1863.

Missionary Society and the African Aid Society, the latter founded in 1860; among the enemies were a large number of British residents in West Africa and the zealous anti-negro pseudo-anthropologists in Britain like Dr. Hunt and Richard Burton, the most vociferous negrophobe foundation members of the Anthropological Society of London.

In Horton's eyes, as in the eyes of leaders of opinion of the first and second generation educated African elite in nineteenth century West Africa, Britain was the effusive lover of Africa, dedicated to the fulfilment of a definite mission in the territory. This mission, as the educated elite conceived it, was to convert its peoples to Christianity, induct them in high-level literary education, transform its customs and institutions and, by science and technology, transform the economy of the territory to the pattern and standard of contemporary Britain. Horton probably expressed the educated Africans' idyllic view of Britain:

> It is an important and universally acknowledged fact, that the greatest friends of the Africans are the philanthropic sons of Britain, and that the Government. . .from whom also they have received paramount blessings, both temporal and spiritual, is the English Government, Africa, therefore, has everything to gain whilst Britannia rules the world. By her squadron she keeps a watchful eye on all those nations who would follow that nefarious practice — the slave trade; her adventurous sons, the missionaries, pierce through the very den of barbarism to become pioneers of civilization. . . . Many have been the means which the English Government has used to raise the condition of the African. This is universally known by every nation, and the African also thoroughly knows and feels it.[22]

This idealisation was not that of a dreamer, for in the third quarter of the nineteenth century there was ample evidence that in the territory British policy substantially reflected that desired by the philanthropists. In embryonic but impressive forms literary education from the primary school

---

22. Horton to Secretary of State for War 13/7/1861 quoted in pp. 46-48 *West African Countries and Peoples*.i,

to university college, industrial institutions, capital investment, African entrepreneurship, British political institutions – were all to be found in British enclaves in West
Africa. In the civil service and Christian mission establishments, the racial prejudice of white competitors notwithstanding, there emerged a small band of educated Africans
who climbed to the top, or very close to the top, of the
greasy pole. One might easily recall Samuel Lewis, who, in
the Legal Department of Sierra Leone, acted as Queen's
Advocate and Chief Justice several times and won a knight-
hood; Dr. J. F. Easmon, who in the Medical Department of
the Gold Coast secured the top post of Chief Medical
Officer in the last decade of the century; Samuel Ajayi
Crowther, who was elevated to full episcopate in Nigeria;
James Quaker and Joseph C. May of Sierra Leone and T. B.
Macaulay and W. Euba of Nigeria, who headed the
secondary grammar schools of Christian missions.

In the Army Medical Department Horton ultimately
climbed very near to the top. In all four enclaves he
occupied high positions of trust and responsibility. In 1862
he was Deputy Assistant Commissary General at Cape
Coast; from 1868 to 1869 he served in the same capacity
in Lagos, apart from holding the posts of Acting Super-
intendent of Stores; from 1872 to 1873 at Sekondi he was
Assistant Commissary and Civil Commandant. He earned
commendation in the military campaigns in which he
participated in the Gold Coast – the Crobboe War (1863)
and the Ashanti Wars (1863 – 1864; 1872 – 1874). In the
latter Ashanti War he received a medal of honour in
addition to special tribute from Earl Carnavon to his
"ability and perseverance in the discharge of a difficult
post".[23] On 5 September, 1879 he was promoted to the
rank of Surgeon Major and was put in charge of the entire
Army Medical Department on the Gold Coast.[24]

23. *West African Reporter* 15/1/1881.
24. Ibid. 10/9/1879.

Horton's three political treatises,[25] of which *Letters on the Political Condition of the Gold Coast* was the last, cannot be fully intelligible to, or appreciated by, present day readers without taking into account his conception of the humanitarian and philanthropic vision of the British presence in West Africa as well as against the background of the political affairs in the lower half of Ghana one hundred years ago.

As Horton perceived, in West Africa the true executors of his vision included Richard Pine, Governor of the Gold Coast from 1862 to 1865, William Blackall and Edward Kennedy, Governors of Sierra Leone from 1866-67 and 1868-72 respectively and Pope Hennessy, Governor-in-Chief of West African Settlements from 1872–73. In Britain the patrons of African progress with whom Horton established contact included the C.M.S., particularly Henry Venn, to whom he dedicated *West African Countries and Peoples* (London, 1868) "as a slight memento of appreciation for his untiring zeal towards the development of the moral, social and Christian advancement of the African Race"; the Education Committee of the War Office, sponsors of his medical training; officials of the War Office and Colonial Office, especially Edward Cardwell, Secretary for War and Earl Granville, Secretary of State for the Colonies, in the Gladstone Government of 1868 to 1874[26] and the African Aid Society.

Of these patrons it was the African Aid Society with which Horton was most closely associated. Under the presidency of Sir Alfred Churchill this unpublicised

25. The two others are worth quoting in full *Political Economy of British Western Africa:* With the Requirements of the several Colonies and Settlements (the African view of the Negro's Place in Nature): being an Address to the African Aid Society London 1865.
   West African Countries and Peoples, British and Native (with the Requirements necessary for Establishing that self-Government recommended by the Committee of the House of Commons, and a vindication of the African Race) London 1868.

26. It was to these two Secretaries that he addressed *Letters on the Political Condition of the Gold Coast.*

organisation served as the arch-defender and relentless advocate of African interests, particularly from 1860 to 1885, forming in the history of humanitarian movement in Britain a link between the Anti-Slave Trade Movement of Wilberforce and Buxton and the Anti-Slavery and Aborigines Protection Society of the post-Scramble era. By memoranda, but largely through its monthly organ, the *African Times*, this organisation attempted to persuade the British Government to expedite the programme drawn up by Henry Venn and endorsed by Horton. So much did Horton appreciate the African Aid Society that in 1864 he initiated African subscription to the funds of the society and appealed with effect to his colleagues in West Africa that the sum of less than £200 for the annual secretariat budget of the organisation should be subscribed by Africans.[27] Through the *African Times*, in which Horton reiterated his views time and again, the society argued forcibly four of the views close to the heart of the African Staff Assistant Surgeon. These were: the necessity of British-type economic revolution for Africa, a refutation of the anti-negro propaganda of the pseudo-anthropologists, Burton and Hunt, the need for raising up an African educated elite leadership, and the advisability of British conquest of the Ashanti for the sake of the Fanti.

Hardly had he arrived on the Gold Coast than Horton began to urge on to agencies of African regeneration the implementation of his vision. Between 1861 and 1863 he invoked the aid of the C.M.S., of the African Aid Society and of Governor Pine in his effort to persuade the Education Committee of the War Office to establish a medical school in West Africa.[28] As he stressed, for many reasons it was expedient that Africans should be trained in

---

27. *African Times*, 23/1/1865.
28. Horton to Secretary for War 13/7/1861 quoted in pp. 46 – 48. *West African Countries and Peoples*. C.M.S. CAI/0117 J. A. Horton to Earl Grey and Lord Ripon 13/11/1863. J. A. Horton to Committee of C.M.S. Committee, 10/12/1863. Governor Pine to Horton, 7/12/1863.

the territory as medical officers. It would be patently a relief to the British Treasury, out of which came the substantial amount of £144 per annum for passages of each European medical officer; it would foster research into African diseases by Africans, the only people qualified to do this by their continuous residence and sense of identification with the territory; lastly and above all the institution would contribute to the experience of Africans for self-government. In order to realise these objectives, declared Horton, the head of the institution must be an African and he must be given a free hand to determine its curriculum from the outset. He offered himself as an African qualified for the post.[29]

His rational scheme did not go beyond the proposition stage. J. T. Brownwell, Commander of Troops, and Charles Callaghan, the Principal Medical Officer, in West Africa, to whom the scheme was sent for observations, killed it. In their opinion the Government had erred by training Africans for the medical profession: medical science was beyond the capacity of the negro. Horton and Davies, they said, were proof of their opinion for, in the words of Callaghan, "neither of the two gentlemen now doing duty on the Gold Coast possess the confidence of the native community in this Territory in the same degree as the European medical officers."[30] No amount of evidence garnered by Horton to expose the prejudice and incorrectness of the comments of the two officers would move the War Office to enter into the scheme.

In the light of the rejection of his scheme as early as 1862 and of his constant awareness that the majority of British residents in West Africa were unyieldingly opposed to sharing, much less conceding, leadership in Church and State to Africans, it might have been expected that Horton's Platonic conception of British presence in West Africa would wane. But this did not happen; the scales did not drop from his eyes in the next decade. As is revealed in

29. C.M.S. CAI/0117 Horton to Earl Grey and Lord Ripon, 13/11/1863.
30. Ibid. Charles Callaghan to Secretary of State for War, 13/12/1861.

bold relief in his nationalistic publications – all of which appeared in the period – he continued to live in hopes and to indulge in incautious optimism, that Britain was consciously committed to transforming West Africa along the British model, economically and socially, and preparing its peoples for independence under the leadership of an African educated elite.

There is no better illustration of Horton's myopia about the nature and purpose of the British mission in West Africa than *Letters on the Political Condition of the Gold Coast*. Territorially the Gold Coast of this publication consisted of only the coastal areas of the Ghana that became independent on 6 March 1957. It was inhabited largely, though not exclusively, by the Fanti branch of the Akan. Although ethnographically they formed a unit with the Ashanti, their neighbour north of the Prah, the two Akan branches, had divergent histories that were to determine their relations with the European powers, particularly the British, in the nineteenth century.

In the seventeenth century the Ashanti clans began to amalgamate and subsequently developed into a formidable power with an extensive empire boasting the umbilical cord of the Golden Stool, around which the unity and solidarity of the Confederacy was galvanised. The paramount King was the Asantahene, who resided at Kumasi, the metropolis. In matters of trade the Ashanti looked more towards Sudan than towards the Atlantic before the eighteenth century. With the aid of a war machine that had begun in this century to instil fear in the European traders on the coast[31] the Ashanti turned their imperial attention toward the coast, crushing and absorbing the Fanti state of Denkyira in the south-west in 1701 and the powerful non-Akan state of Akyem in the south-east in 1740.

Fanti history was rather different. Not only did the tribes refuse to amalgamate; they constantly warred against one another. Not even the advent of European traders of

31. George Nφrregard, *Danish Settlements in West Africa 1658-1850* (translated by Sigurd Mammem) Boston 1966. p. 102

different nationalities from the fifteenth century onwards would persuade them to close their ranks and appreciate the inherent danger posed by European presence to the sovereignty and territorial integrity of Fantiland. By allying with one faction against the other the European powers found little difficulty in fanning the flames of hostility between one Fanti state and another, in their own interests. In such circumstances neither the will nor the power to combine against the European intruders on the Atlantic seaboard or the Ashanti imperial threat existed. Although the ruler of Mankessim was regarded by all the Fanti kings as a kind of *primus inter pares* he was not in the pivotal position of the Asantahene, nor did Abura, a sort of Fanti capital, evoke the centrepetal appeal of Kumasi. The result was that at the height of the trans-Atlantic slave trade there were not less than thirty-two forts (out of a total of forty-three for all West Africa) on the Gold Coast alone, owned by the English, the Dutch, the Danes and the Bradenburghers. These forts — many of them massive fortifications — became *de facto* independent enclaves whence the European occupants, regarded by the African chiefs as tenants at will, defied the authority of the traditional rulers with impunity and dabbled in local politics.

By the first decade of the nineteeth century, when several European countries abolished the trans-Atlantic slave trade, the British, the Dutch and the Danes remained fort-owners on the Gold Coast. Of these three it was the British, who bought out the Danes in 1851 as they were to buy out the Dutch in 1872, that retained an imperial interest, first in the economic sphere and subsequently in territorial terms. Up to 1807 the Company of Merchants Trading to Africa which had been in charge of British interest in the slave trade and in political rivalry with the other European powers for more than three centuries, received a subsidy of £13,000 per annum for the mainten-ance of the English forts of Dixcove, Cape Coast, Anamaboe and Accra. To compensate for the loss in profit from the slave trade the subsidy was increased to £20,000 per annum up to 1821. In that year the forts were taken over by the Colonial Office, until 1828 when their custody was again transferred to a group of merchants, Committee of Merchants of London, with a subsidy of £4,000. For the next fifteen years British influence in the Gold Coast increased enormously under the non-legal but nonetheless effectual rule of the famous George Maclean.

As President of the Council of Merchants at Cape Coast, the administrative organ of the Committee of Merchants of London, George Maclean added Fantiland to the informal empire of Britain. Not only did the British settle disputes between Fanti states but they attempted to make laws for the Fanti. This African people, it began to be said, fell within the British Protectorate; the Fanti, in turn, had begun to look to Britain as their protector. Not that the Fanti wished to surrender their sovereignty and territory to the British; all they wanted, and craved for, was that the military power of Britain should act as a deterrent to the Ashanti, for they feared that the Ashanti were bent upon their destruction. In other words the Fanti saw and valued the British mainly as an instrument for the furtherance of their own exclusive interests. But the belief of the Fanti that they could employ the terror of British presence to provoke the Ashanti with impunity, was to have serious consequences for all.

As it seemed to the Fanti, Anglo-Ashanti relations in the half a century after British abolition of the slave trade justified their belief and interpretation of the purpose of British presence on the Gold Coast. For between 1807 and 1863, often as a result of acts of provocation by the Fanti, the British and Ashanti resorted to armed conflicts in which victory oscillated — going to the British in 1807 and 1831, to the Ashanti in 1824 and 1863.[32] And there is no doubt that the military capacity of the British, or rather its

32. For a comprehensive survey of Anglo-Ashanti relations see W. W. Claridge *A History of the Gold Coast and Ashanti* 2 Vols. 2nd Edition Frank Cass 1964.

role as a deterrent, saved the Fanti from forcible absorption into the Ashanti empire in the nineteenth century.

Nevertheless the British did not see themselves exactly in the way the Fanti saw them — as primarily, guarantors and defenders of the interests and independence of the Fanti against the Ashanti. Britain only *appeared* to be drawing the chestnut out of the fire for the Fanti. British hatred for, and armed conflict with, the Ashanti was determined primarily, if not exclusively, first by British economic interests and later by imperial ambition. It required no imagination for the British to perceive that to allow the Ashanti to extend their sway over the coastal areas would eventually mean dealing with a virile African power which could not be frightened into submitting to British wishes; that could hold its own in economic and diplomatic negotiations; and that would not brook British interference in domestic matters. It was clear to the British that the Ashanti, if allowed to gravitate towards the coast, would be as hostile as the Egba and the Ijebu of contemporary Yorubaland and, if need be, attempt to starve British trade out of the Gold Coast in order to check Britain's menacing imperial presence. By keeping the Fanti away from the Ashanti orbit the British derived enormous economic advantages. For without any sort of treaties British trade was carried on freely and safely throughout the "Protectorate", a situation which derived from the fact that the Fanti were within the British orbit. No such condition favourable to the British existed in any other part of West Africa, hence the fire and sword which in the last decade of the nineteenth century the British brought upon the heads of the peoples who would not open their roads to unfettered British trade.

Horton and the African Aid Society became relentless and prejudiced exponents of the interests of the Fanti and assumed a decidedly belligerent anti-Ashanti tone in their propaganda. There was no question of learning or understanding the history of the Ashanti with impartiality. He took sides with the Fanti, perhaps more instinctively than consciously. For unlike the Ashanti, who were absolutely and deliberately impervious to European influence, which they regarded as inimical to themselves, the Fanti seemed to Horton a people disposed to share his vision of a new Africa. They welcomed Christian missions; they began to patronise Western forms of education, apart from industrial training which flourished best among them in the whole of West Africa under the encouragement of the Basel missionaries; they began to plant coffee for export; they were pro-British in their sentiment; they welcomed foreign sojourners; they were prepared to be tutored in the constitutional pattern of Britain.

Although *Letters on the Political Condition of the Gold Coast* contains here and there allusions to his visionary programme for West Africa in general, the main theme with which it deals is the Fanti interest in the Gold Coast. It is the Fanti viewpoint which Horton analyses in some detail on the two major issues – the Anglo-Dutch agreement of 1867 and the Fanti Confederation – that feature in the nine letters which make the book. In respect of the former, Horton was embittered that contrary to Fanti interest, rather than buying the Dutch out of the Gold Coast, the British transferred Fanti inhabitants of some British forts who were ultra-loyalist to the British, to the Dutch, in the treaty of exchange of territories. In respect of the Fanti Confederation Horton was incensed that rather than taking the bull by the horns, the British had, against the Fanti interest, changed their attitude to the Ashanti; on the contrary, he was concerned with persuading the British Government to patronise the Confederation as the beginning of implementation of a policy of creation of a series of West African nations.

It was to his intense mortification that in 1867 the Dutch and the English negotiated and signed the treaty by which they exchanged territories. The division among the Fanti had been accentuated by the way in which forts were held between the Dutch and the British along the coast from Appolonia in the west to the Volta in the east. These positions were not continuous but intermingled, Dutch with English. Naturally over the years inhabitants were loyal to their respective colonial masters, the Fanti in British forts to the British, those in Dutch forts to the Dutch.

The two European powers did not pursue similar policies. The British were, for instance, anti-Ashanti, the Dutch, with their chief fort at Elmina, perpetual allies of the Ashanti; the British levied small *ad valorem* customs duties on imports in their possession for the purpose of establishing and maintaining an administration and they encouraged educational establishments. In contrast the Dutch did not levy any customs duties whatever; nor could they boast of agencies for the social improvement of the people in their possessions. The whole charge for the Dutch establishments, which cost from £10,000 to £12,000 per annum, was borne by Holland. In return for this financial burden, the Dutch, it is said, recruited three hundred Fanti every year ostensibly for military service in Java.[33]

Horton hated the idea of continued Dutch presence on the Gold Coast.[34] He wanted the Union Jack alone to wave over the entire coast from Appolonia to the Volta, in the belief, which was to be shared later by nationalists in colonial British West Africa, that the British were the most humane, the most paternal and the most truly devoted promoters of the intrinsic interests of the Africans. So blind was Horton that he affected to believe that in contrast to the inhabitants of British possessions those in Dutch possessions had never admired Dutch rule and only too eagerly and gratefully accepted British suzerainty.

In order to exorcise Dutch presence from the Gold Coast the African Aid Society suggested to the British Government that they should pay them anything from £50,000 to £100,000. However, it was feared that Parliament would not entertain such an expenditure which did not look like a sound investment. In order to enable the British to earn more revenue and consolidate their admini-

33. *African Times* 23/4/1868
34. Below p. 140.

stration, attempts were made to persuade the Dutch to level uniform duties with the British. But it was to no avail. Only one proposal was acceptable to Holland – that of exchange of territories in such a way that the Dutch would control Appolonia to Elmina and the British the rest to the Volta.

This treaty, which was ratified on 5 July, 1867 and put into effect on 1 January 1868, was negotiated without any consultation with the inhabitants. The matter was kept so secret that the people involved on the British side were not informed until only a few days before the transfer took place. Naturally they were stupefied that they were to be transferred like goods and chattels in a house, "fixtures and furnitures included"[35] to a power they had been brought up to hate. In exasperation they translated their anti-Dutch feelings into physical demonstrations and took the law into their hands, in the hope that the British would appreciate the strength of their loyalty to the British empire and cancel their treaty obligations. However, as the inhabitants of British Kommenda learned to their misfortune, they had miscalculated. In the presence of the British Governor they were awarded an exemplary punishment, involving loss of lives and property by their new Dutch masters!

The whole episode was extremely mortifying to Horton. In his judgment the British had renounced the moral obligation which, he had always believed, they had towards the Fanti loyalists. His bitterness at what he considered a shameful abnegation of duties, a policy of blundering and thundering by the British, is clear from this book. However, what is not available in these letters – and what is of crucial significance – is that the Anglo-Dutch agreement marked a parting of the ways between him and the African Aid Society. For the latter, although the treaty was not ideal, from the viewpoint of British commercial prospects, it was, in the words of the Society's organ, "a great step made towards future good government, towards the more rapid development of the great material resources of

35. *African Times*, 23/8/1867.

countries now included within the British boundaries." It poignantly declared further, "We have before us an agreeable vista of improved facilities for embarking and disembarking products and goods; of steam power on the River Volta; of canalised water — courses for irrigation; of cotton, coffee, indigo, oil-seed, and sugar plantations, & co & co, with many other things that come with these and follow in their track." The human factor — the African side of the matter — which was the primary concern of Horton, was ignored. As they admitted: "we are not going to make a special African grievance of this."[36]

It was a traumatic experience for Horton. It was not until now that he was shocked out of his illusions to perceive that the interests of Africans and those of avowed humanitarian organisations sponsored in Britain by interested economic directors were not necessarily at all times identical. Horton's experience and shock anticipated those that awaited African nationalists of the pre-World War I West Africa, who mistakenly thought that there was an identity of interests and purpose between themselves and the British Anti-Slavery and Aborigines Protection Society.

Whilst he was vituperating against what he considered to be British betrayal of the trust reposed in them by the Fanti it seemed to him that a new era was dawning in Fantiland. For the first time in their history a feeling of togetherness came upon this people; they felt the need to combine as a nation in the interest of national survival; they formed the Fanti Confederation.

The Fanti Confederation, it should be stressed, was a child of necessity and not a product of a process of education or organic growth in the vision of Horton. Its origins go back to 1863-4 when the Fanti discovered for the first time that the British protectorship, which they had assumed existed for their benefit and which they considered to be a prescriptive right in all their dealings with the Ashanti, might not be available whenever they wished after

36. Ibid.

all. When in 1863 the British forces were humiliated on the battlefield by the Ashanti, rather than avenge the humiliation, the British Government recoiled and several politicians in England began to plead for complete political withdrawal from the Gold Coast. The desire of Governor Pine, like the hawks, Horton and the African Aid Society, for a total military crushing of the Ashanti, once and for all, was over-ruled by what the interpreters of British interest in Westminster considered to be the true interests of the British in West Africa. Under the spell of the Manchester School doctrine, that colonies were a millstone around Britain's neck, officials at the Colonial Office, too, began to assess the exclusive British interest in West Africa. The climate of opinion was such that the possessions in West Africa were felt politically and administratively to be an incubus. Britain, it was contended, did not have to erect an administration there to achieve its main objective — profitable trade. For, as the Commission of Inquiry sent out to the territory in 1865[37] to ascertain British interests declared, British trade was most successful in the Niger Delta where there was no colonial administrative apparatus, where interference in the purely local politics did not have to inflame African feelings against an unwanted foreign establishment — as British establishment on the Gold Coast seemed to the Ashanti. In rational terms, then, it was forcibly argued that British interest demanded non-involvement in the unsavoury interior politics. In the famous language of the Select Committee of the House of Commons, Britain's aim in West Africa should be gradual withdrawal "with the possible exception of Sierra Leone."[38]

Horton and the Fanti were stunned that the British Government had proved a broken reed, leaving the Fanti in the lurch to sort out their relations with the Ashanti and work out their own salvation. Their answer to the Ashanti

37. Parliamentary Paper 1865, V(412) *Report of Select Committee on State of British Settlements on the West Coast of Africa.*
38. Ibid.

problem was the Fanti Confederation which had a fragile existence of less than five years. Horton himself was not involved in the formation and activities of the organisation, the details of which have been treated comprehensively elsewhere.[39] His concern was to see the organisation survive, to persuade the British to be favourably disposed towards it and to treat it as a Charter of Independence and Nationhood for the Fanti as well as a beginning in the formation of the British-sponsored West African nations of his dream. In this book Horton provides an ideological justification for the existence of the Fanti Confederation to a degree in many ways significant in the study of the evolution of African Political Theory in West Africa in the last one-hundred years.

The Fanti Confederation was one of the earliest efforts by the African educated elite to seize the initiative in political leadership, through co-operation with traditional rulers. Only a few years earlier and in quite different circumstances — in the Ẹgba capital of Abẹokuta — George William Johnson, a *Saro* like Horton, had persuaded the Ẹgba rulers to agree to the formation of the Ẹgba United Board of Management, under the leadership of the educated elite.[40]

As part of his enchantment with British culture and institutions, Horton was hypnotised by British political ideas to the extent that he lacked an understanding of traditional African political system. In a way that present day political scientists and social anthropologists would find astonishing, he denied to Africans the capacity for political systems and ideas in "primitive" West Africa.[41] As he said the territory was immersed in "utter barbarism" until the European "civilisers" began their mission in the nineteenth century.[42] Concerning the Constitution by which society in

39. David Kimble, *A Political History of Ghana* (The Rise of Gold Coast Nationalism 1850 — 1928) O.U.P. 1963 pp. 222–263.
40. J. M. Kopytoff, *A Preface to Modern Nigeria* Madison 1965. pp. 178-181.
41. J. A. B. Horton, *West African Countries and Peoples* pp. 1–11
42. Ibid. p. 28

"primitive" Africa was governed Horton made the mistake, characteristic of uninformed and jaundiced European writers of his age, of believing that unmitigated and unenlightened despotism was not only possible in human society but was typical of the African continent. Hence Horton's hope that through the Fanti Confederation, the British would begin to enlighten West African nations "in the true principles of a civilized Government."[43]

The bias he had in favour of the educated elite, and against the traditional rulers, was natural. He had the vision of a West Africa in which unlettered chiefs and society would be things of the past; in which literacy would be the *sine qua non* for directorship of government; in which meritocracy, in literary and technological terms, would replace leadership by hereditary class. As he said: "The political constitution of the interior tribes on the Gold Coast is of a very primitive order, and their social organisation resembles most closely the feudal system of Europe in the middle ages."[44] In elation he saw all this "tottering to its foundation" and the new order of a British model Constitution and the educated elite already evolving.

Horton believed that the triumph of the educated elite could be achieved by the end of the nineteenth century, that if the British set their mind to it the educated elite would have complete control of all the governments of the British possessions of West Africa.[45] By 1893, he said, the Gambia could become self-governing under a popularly elected "enlightened" native king. In Sierra Leone, within a much shorter time, a monarchical system — the king to be elected by universal suffrage — could be easily put into effect. On the Gold Coast the Fanti should have at the apex of their government a "King of Fantee", to be appointed by universal suffrage. He went out of his way to suggest the name of Honourable George Blankson, a nominated African unofficial member of the Gold Coast

43. Below p. 151
44. Below p. 149
45. J. A. B. Horton, *West African Countries and Peoples.* pp. 75–135

Legislative Council, as a man who would be acceptable to all Fanti as their "King".[46]

As historians of West Africa know very well the authority and power of the traditional rulers did not immediately collapse; they did not abdicate their sovereignty in the easy manner which Horton had assumed would occur in the case of the Fanti Confederation. In the Gold Coast, as in all West Africa, the so-called natural rulers did not see themselves as subordinates playing second fiddle to the educated elite. As the history of nationalism on the Gold Coast was to prove, until 1920, when Casely Hayford, an educated Fanti, founded the National Congress of British West Africa, the educated elite looked upon the chiefs as patrons and financial sponsors.[47] Even after 1920, as the tension between Nana Sir Ofori Attah and Nnamdi Azikiwe in the thirties, and between aristocratic Dr. J. B. Danquah and proletarian Kwame Nkrumah in the forties, showed that the traditional chiefs and aristocracy did not wish to relinquish leadership or leave unchallenged the attempts of the *parvenu* educated elite to undermine and efface the claims of the hereditary aristocracy.[48]

But although Horton's dream of the social and political revolution of West Africa was not to occur with the ease, suddenness and immediacy he desired − and he wanted the British to see through this revolution in respect of the Confederation − yet his views on the Fanti Confederation are significant in one other respect. They constitute a part of his nationalist outlook which should be taken into account in the literature of the emergence of African nationalism. In a sense the Fanti Confederation was, in his view, a fulfilment of the hope cherished in a resolution of the 1865 Select Committee, that Africans were to be left to govern themselves.[49]

46. Ibid. p. 126
47. David Kimble op. cit. p. 389 ff
48. Nnamdi Azikiwe *Renascent Africa*, Lagos 1937; reprinted Frank Cass 1968, p 21 f
49. Below p. 8; p. 151 ff

For much as Horton desired to see the British flag waving over extending frontiers in West Africa — and he never actually stated categorically that Britain should ever withdraw completely — the ideal situation he envisaged, was a West Africa of independent sovereign nations, but with the British as a sort of god-father. It would be mistaken to dismiss Horton as an imperialist agent, in spite of his mental and cultural enslavement by British codes and culture.

Indeed in the sixties, with the possible exception of Edward Blyden, no contemporary was able to stand up to Burton and Hunt, in defence of the claim of the Negro Race to common humanity and the organic equality of Africans with other races. Horton rejoiced that the African climate was hostile to the white man; that, on account of this, "tropical Africa must be left eventually for the Africans";[50] that on their continent, Africans, with the opportunity of contact with the world of learning, science and technology would establish nations which, in time, "will occupy a prominent position in the world's history, and when they will command a voice in the council of nations."[51] It was in this light that Horton has in this book painted the Fanti Confederation in very romantic terms; he viewed the organisation with unbridled optimism, idealising its possibilities in a manner quite unrelated to facts, indulging in, and optimistic about untried hopes in the capacity of the Fanti to achieve a Westminster-type democracy, and accepting the social revolution of his dream.

It was not long before Horton's hopes and idealism about the Fanti Confederation crashed like a house of cards. The British had since 1866 changed their attitude to the Gold Coast, indicating that they would neither withdraw nor encourage African independence movements.[52] They were not only determined to stay on, but they

50. I. A. B. Horton, *West African Countries and Peoples* p. 72
51. Ibid. p. VIII
52. David Kimble, Op. cit. pp. 192-221.

intended to spread their imperial tentacles farther and farther into the interior, effacing in British interests the pre-Scramble African nations like Ashanti, Gonja and Dagomba. In 1872 the Dutch were bought out of the Gold Coast. Two years later the Ashanti were smashed, and the Gold Coast, which Horton desired to see as an independent Fanti nation, was formally incorporated into the British Empire.

By 1874 the Fanti Confederation had been murdered by the British administration. As the *African Times* had editorialised as early as 23 November 1871, "if not asleep, it (the Confederation) has at least been too much in the shade." The British administration did not conceal its hostility to the organisation. It was quite natural that the British should not see themselves as sponsors of political organisations, the aim of which was to terminate their rule.

Indeed Horton did not escape the hostility of some British officials on the Gold Coast, who questioned the propriety of his exposition and defence of the interests of the Fanti.[53] As a civil servant he was lucky to have escaped censure for airing in his publications such opinions and making such exposures which discredited individual British officers and criticised British policies.

Presumably because officialdom frowned on his articulateness, from 1870 onwards, Horton remained taciturn for the rest of his life. He no longer expressed any political views; he ceased to be a correspondent of the *African Times*; he subscribed no views, not a word, to the *Gold Coast Times*, which was founded in the seventies. He retired on a pension in December 1880.

For the rest of his life Horton turned his attention to economic affairs. Not that he had not been expressing views on the economic development of West Africa; since the sixties he had emphasied that, for him, the pace of commercial and industrial growth of the territory had been too slow.[54] The political and social revolution of his vision,

53. Ibid. p. 245
54. See *Political Economy of British Western Africa* cited Page 20.

he appreciated, could not occur except in the context of a sophisticated European-type industrial environment. Hence the emphasis of his educational proposals on science and technology. As he declared in this publication, "the *material advancement of the people*" should be a primary aim of the British in West Africa.[55] He spilled considerable ink urging the need for scientific farming and went to the extent of studying the soils of the Gold Coast. Properly tutored, he affirmed, West Africa could grow both for home consumption and for export, coffee, tea and chicory.[56]

In practical terms it was after his retirement that he became involved in business. On the Gold Coast, he held several Directorships including those of the Wassaw Light Railway Company Limited and Wassaw and Ahanta Gold Mines Syndicate Limited. But it is his pioneering effort in banking that is most noteworthy.

In December 1882 he founded the Commercial Bank of West Africa. Although the bank was still at its infancy when death claimed Horton in October 1883, he had made history as the architect of banking in the territory, since his bank was the first practical proposition in banking in West Africa. As early as 1872 the Messrs Child, Mills and Company of Sierra Leone had announced the formation of a "Bank of West Africa", but it was still-born. In June and September 1881 two attempts were made — again by Europeans — but, as then alleged, these attempts did not go beyond the proposal stage because European firms feared that these banks might make credit facilities available to rival Africans. Such credit facilities, the European firms had always feared, would put their African rivals in direct touch with the English manufacturers. The fourth attempt made in August 1882 to found the "London and West African Bank" with a capital of £500,000 suffered a similar fate.[57]

In the circumstances only an African could break through the monopoly and stranglehold of the European

55. Below p. 138
56. *African Times* Africanus Horton, "African Products"
57. *West African Reporter* 10/3/1883.

traders by founding an indigenous bank. Horton took this step. It was an individual and private undertaking with headquarters at Shaftesbury House, Freetown, and branches at Barthurst, Cape Coast Castle and Lagos. His bankers in Britain were Messrs Sir C. McGrigor, Bart. and Company of 25 Charles Street, St James' Square, London. Horton himself was the Manager and Director.[58] The aim was to make credit facilities available to African traders on the guarantee of Horton's social standing and the wealth he was believed to have acquired. The bank actually came into operation and was reported to be doing quite well when death swept Horton away at 9 p.m. 15 October, 1883, after a short illness.

Horton's claim to attention today by Africanists is manifold. Intellectuals who care to read his political treatises would find pleasure in his serene and unemotional style and his scientific analysis; medical historians would find his researches into guinea-worm and the effects of West African climate on human health rewarding; medical students would not be wasting their time by perusing his learned articles in the *Athenaeum,* the *Lancet,* the *Medical Press and Circular* and the *Medical Times and Gazette.* Pan-Africanists would find refreshing his cosmopolitanism of outlook. Above all, Africans, pessimistic about the future of their continent and sceptical about the mental and moral endowments of their race, may find an inspiration in his unstinted optimism about Africa and Africans.

Department of History,   E. A. Ayandele
University of Ibadan,
Ibadan.
31 July, 1968.

58. *African Times*, 1/12/1882.

Published by Subscription for Private Circulation only.

LETTERS

ON THE

POLITICAL CONDITION OF THE GOLD COAST

SINCE THE EXCHANGE OF TERRITORY BETWEEN THE

ENGLISH AND DUTCH GOVERNMENTS, ON JANUARY 1, 1868;

TOGETHER WITH A SHORT ACCOUNT OF

THE ASHANTEE WAR, 1862-4, AND THE AWOONAH WAR, 1866;

ADDRESSED TO THE RIGHT HON. E. CARDWELL, D.C.L.,

SECRETARY OF STATE FOR WAR; AND

THE RIGHT HON. EARL GRANVILLE, K.G., D.C.L.,

SECRETARY OF STATE FOR THE COLONIES.

BY AFRICANUS B. HORTON,

M.D. EDIN., F.R.G.S.,

Author of "Political Economy of British Western Africa, with the Requirements of the Several Colonies and Settlements;" "Physical and Medical Climate and Meteorology of Western Africa;" "West African Countries and People, British and Natives; and a Vindication of the Negro Race;" "Guinea Worm, or Dracunculus: its Symptoms, Progress, Causes, Pathological Anatomy, Results, and Radical Cure;" &c., &c., &c. ; Staff Assistant-Surgeon of Her Majesty's Forces in West Africa ; Associate of King's College, London ; Foreign Fellow of the Botanical Society of Edinburgh ; Corresponding Member of the Medical Society of King's College, London ; Late President of the Pathological Society of Edinburgh ; Fellow of the Noetic Society of Edinburgh ; Member of the Institute d'Afrique of Paris, &c., &c., &c.

LONDON:

WILLIAM JOHN JOHNSON, 121, FLEET STREET, E.C.

1870.

TO

SIR ARTHUR EDWARD KENNEDY C.B.

Governor-General

OF

HER BRITANNIC MAJESTY'S POSSESSIONS

ON THE

WEST COAST OF AFRICA,

&c.,   &c.,   &c.,

This Work,

IS MOST RESPECTFULLY DEDICATED,

AS A TRIBUTE OF SINCERE RESPECT,

BY

THE AUTHOR.

LIST OF SUBSCRIPTIONS FOR "LETTERS ON GOLD COAST POLITICS."

CAPE COAST.

	£	s.	d.
Colonial Government	5	5	0
H. T. Ussher, Esq., Administrator	2	2	0
Mr. F. C. Grant	2	2	0
„ Wm. C. Finlayson	2	2	0
„ H. F. Blissett, Commissariat	1	1	0
„ C. C. Brown	1	1	0
„ W. D. Howson	1	1	0
„ Samuel Davis	1	1	0
„ W. Cleaver	1	1	0
„ J. Hill Capper	1	1	0
„ F. E. Bennett	1	1	0
„ W. R. Taylor	1	2	6
„ Edmund Bannerman	1	1	0
„ W. R. Wade	1	1	0
„ R. G. Leighton	1	1	0
„ E. Fiddes, Lieut. 1st W.I. Regiment ...	1	0	0
„ H. F. Morgue	1	0	0
„ John Grant	0	10	6
„ W. E. Davidson	0	10	6
„ Alfred Triggs	0	10	6
„ C. Bartels	0	10	6
Sergeant Henry Bourke	0	10	6
Rev. M. Grimmer	0	10	6
Mr. Hastings Kneller	0	10	6
„ Mr. J. Bell, Ensign 1st W.I. Regiment ...	0	10	0
„ James H. Brew	0	10	6
„ C. S. Salmon	1	1	0

List of Subscriptions from other parts had not been received
when this was forwarded to the Printers.

PREFACE.

"ROME was not built in a day;" the proudest
kingdom in Europe was once in a state of barbarism
perhaps worse than now exists amongst the tribes
chiefly inhabiting the West Coast of Africa ; and it
is an incontrovertible axiom that what has been done
can again be done. If Europe, therefore, has been
raised to her present pitch of civilization by progressive advancement, Africa too, with a guarantee
of the civilization of the north, will rise into equal
importance. The nucleus has been planted; it is
just beginning to show signs of life and future
vigour; it shoots out legitimate as well as extraneous
buds. Political capital is made of the latter by
narrow-minded persons ; whilst the liberal-minded,
with more philosophy and generosity, make ample
allowances for these defects, and encourage the
legitimate growth. We may well say that the present state of Western Africa is, in fact, the history
of the world repeating itself.

The civilization of France and England, and even of Germany, dates from the time when Rome, agitated by social contentions, made Julius Cæsar proconsul of Transalpine Gaul ; the brilliant conquest which he made over the then savage tribes, who lived in caves and miserable huts, and the wise but rigid government which he enforced, led in eleven hundred years to the gigantic discoveries and improvements which now startle the denizens of less favoured climes.

But I argue that modern inventions, such as printing, steam agency (both as regards railways and navigation), and the electric telegraph, which facilitate rapid communication in a most wonderful degree, leave not a shadow of doubt in my mind that, although it took eleven hundred years to bring France and England to the high standard of civilization which they now occupy, it will take far less time to bring a portion at least of Western Africa to vie with Europe in progressive development. Descended from the royal blood of Isuama Eboe, and having had ample opportunities, from close acquaintance with almost all forms of government exercised in the most important countries in the western part of Africa, of judging of the influence

of civilization in modern times on races of different
and most opposite character, I have hazarded the
above opinion, and I am certain that those who have
made this view the subject of sober consideration
will bear me out in the statement.

On this Coast the English element is unquestion-
ably the best civilizing agency. Their liberality in
matters of Christianity, their sound and healthy
judgment in colonization, their profound legislative
ability, exhibited frequently in adopting proper
means to suit the wishes and desires of the colonists,
and their commercial policy, all greatly tend to
foster the growth of civilization in a young colony.
Occasionally, however, we meet with a few who find
their way to the Coast, who endeavour to the utmost
of their ability to undo what the well-disposed have
done ; but this must be regarded as the constant
concomitant of progressive improvement in the
early history of every country, when the civilizing
agency comes from abroad.

The following is the Convention between Her
Majesty and the King of the Netherlands for an
interchange of territory on the Gold Coast of
Africa, signed at London, March 5, 1867 ; Ratifications exchanged at London, July 5, 1867 :—

Her Majesty the Queen of the United Kingdom of Great Britain and Ireland, and His Majesty the King of the Netherlands, being of opinion that an interchange of territory on the West Coast of Africa would conduce to their mutual advantage, and would promote the interests of the inhabitants, have resolved to conclude a convention for that purpose, and have therefore named as their plenipotentiaries, that is to say—(here follow the names of the plenipotentiaries)—who, after having communicated to each other their respective full powers, found in good and due form, have agreed upon the following articles :—

ARTICLE I. Her Britannic Majesty cedes to his Majesty the King of the Netherlands all British forts, possessions, and rights of sovereignty or jurisdiction which she possesses on the Gold Coast westward of the mouth of the Sweet River, where their respective territories are conterminous ; and his Majesty the King of the Netherlands cedes to her Britannic Majesty all Netherland forts, possessions, and rights of sovereignty or jurisdiction which he possesses on the Gold Coast to the eastward of the mouth of the Sweet River, where their respective territories are conterminous. The boundary between the possessions of her Britannic Majesty and those of his Majesty the King of the Netherlands will be a line drawn true north from the centre of the mouth of the Sweet River, as far as the boundary of the present Ashantee kingdom, but with such deviations within three English miles of the coast as shall be necessary to retain within British territory any villages which have been in habitual dependence on the British Government at Cape Coast, and within Netherland territory any villages which have been in habitual dependence on the Netherland Government at St. George d'Elmina.

ARTICLE II. The two high contracting parties agree that the following tariff of duties of customs shall be enforced in their respective possessions upon the Gold Coast :—

In the British Possessions: ale, beer, wine, and all spirits or spirituous liquors, per old wine gallon, sixpence ; cigars, snuff, or tobacco in any shape, per pound, one penny ; gunpowder, per pound, one penny; firearms of every description, each, one shilling; on all other goods of every kind, an *ad valorem* duty of 3 per cent. on the invoice price.

In the Netherland Possessions : ale, beer, wine, and all spirits or spirituous liquors, per litre, eight cents; cigars, snuff, or tobacco, in any shape, per kilogramme, ten cents; gunpowder, per kilogramme, ten cents; firearms of every description, each, sixty cents; on all other goods of every kind, an *ad valorem* duty of three per cent. on the invoice price.

ARTICLE III.   In order to prevent frauds in the importation of goods, the high contracting parties engage to empower the officers of their respective customs on the Gold Coast to require the masters of vessels to make declaration of the nature, quantity, and value of any goods which they may be allowed to land.   If the officers of customs shall be of opinion that the value so to be declared is insufficient, they shall be at liberty to take the goods on public account, on paying to the importer the amount of his valuation, with the addition of 10 per cent. thereon, and returning any duty which may have been already paid.

ARTICLE IV.   The tariff of customs duties specified in Article II. shall be put into operation from and after a day to be agreed upon between the two Governments, and shall remain in force for a period of ten years; and further, until the expiration of twelve months after either of the two contracting parties shall have given notice to the other of its desire for a revision or termination thereof.

ARTICLE V.   The tariff of customs duties may be enforced or relaxed by the local authorities at their own discretion, or according to the orders of their respective Governments in respect of articles imported for the use of those authorities, or for the personal use and consumption of officers in the actual service of the Government.

ARTICLE VI.   The mutual transfer of forts, possessions, and rights of sovereignty or jurisdiction, stipulated in Article I. of the present convention, is dependent upon and subject to the establishment of the proposed tariff, and shall not take effect until the Government of each country shall have procured the enactment of any laws or regulations necessary in order to establish that tariff for the term and under the conditions hereinbefore described, and shall have actually put the same into operation.

ARTICLE VII. After the transfer alluded to in the foregoing Article shall have been made, a map shall be drawn of the new boundary division according to the terms of Article I. Two copies of the said map, duly attested by the Governments on either side, shall then be appended to this convention for the purpose of show-ing the boundary, which shall undergo no alteration, even should any of the villages mentioned at the end of Article I. be subsequently abandoned or the tariff be modified or withdrawn.

ARTICLE VIII. The present convention, after receiving so far as may be necessary the approval of the legislative authority, shall be ratified, and the ratifications shall be exchanged at London within a period of four months, or sooner if possible.

In witness whereof the respective plenipotentiaries have signed the same, and have affixed thereto the seals of their arms.

Done at London, the fifth day of March, in the year of our Lord one thousand eight hundred and sixty seven.

CARNARVON.   BENTINCK.

STANLEY.   C. J. M. NAGTGLAS.

J. A. B. HORTON, M.D.,

Staff Assistant-Surgeon

Cape Coast Castle,

May 16, 1870.

CIRCULAR INTRODUCTION.

THE history of a country forms a part of the history of the world, and its publication is necessary for its preservation. Thus Cæsar preserved his brilliant conquests over the Gauls in his Commentaries, and Cicero the glorious history of the Roman Republic in his voluminous writings.

With the view of preserving in a continuous form the history of the Gold Coast for the last ten years, I have in a series of correspondence with the Right Hon. Edward Cardwell, D.C.L., Secretary of State for War, and Earl Granville, K.G., D.C.L., Secretary of State for the Colonies, given a full account of the political atmosphere of the Gold Coast a few years prior to and since the transfer of territory between the English and Dutch Governments, justifying the British Fantees under existing circumstances in refusing to acknowledge the Dutch flag, recounting the outrages at Commendah, the formation of the Fantee Confederation, the victorious attack on Elmina by the Fantee force, the inglorious campaign against the Ashantees under Major Cochrane and Lieutenant-Colonel

Conran, the Accra native Confederation, the Awoonah War, the bombardment of Dixcove, the atrocious march of Atjiempon from Asinee through the Dutch territory into Elmina, the Dutch capital, and the means necessary for placing the country in a more satisfactory state.

It is, perhaps, needless to state that it has cost me about two hundred and fifty pounds for publishing works on Western Africa, which I am proud to say have been, and I hope will be of future benefit to the Coast. Considering with what little interest people in civilized countries regard subjects on Africa, works on Western Africa, unless written to attract the fancy or to excite wonder, by recording acts of heroic enterprise, like the gorilla hunting, &c., are a dead loss to the writer.

I intend, therefore, to publish these communications for private circulation only. It is likely to cost from £30 to £40. As it is for the future benefit of a part of Western Africa, I ask those who have the interest of the country at heart to subscribe something towards that expense. Several copies will be forwarded gratis to subscribers, and all subscriptions will be acknowledged in the work by

AFRICANUS HORTON.

LETTERS ON THE POLITICAL CONDITION OF THE GOLD COAST.

LETTER No. I.*

TO THE RIGHT HON. EDWARD CARDWELL, HER MAJESTY'S SECRETARY OF STATE FOR WAR.

CAPE COAST CASTLE,
12th August, 1869.

MY DEAR SIR,

In my work on the "West African Countries and People, British and Native, with the Requirements necessary for Establishing that Self-Government recommended by the Committee of the House of Commons in 1865, and a Vindication of the Negro Race," which I had the honour of personally presenting to you in July, 1868, I endeavoured to point out, as succinctly as possible, in pages 246 to 250, how utterly one-sided was the exchange of territory between the Dutch and Eng-

---

* Reply dated 11th October, and marked " Private."

B

lish on the Gold Coast, as represented in the treaty
signed by the plenipotentiaries of both countries on
6th March, 1867, and ratified on 6th July, 1867.
And in that interview I entered fully on the feelings
of the people, especially those who had been transferred to the Dutch authorities, without their being
consulted ; how that, at the time, they declared
that, being under British protection, and not British
subjects, they had a right to be heard on the
subject ; that most of the transferred subjects would
not tolerate the Dutch rule ; and that troubles were
looming in the distance, which could only be averted
by great conciliation and courteous behaviour on
the part of the Dutch Government to those who
were to be transferred.

As the political state of the Gold Coast has been
one of feverish excitement for the last two years,
and as every month seems to bring fresh matters
tending to agitate the public mind, I purpose to
give you, in this and subsequent communications,
as complete a statement as I can of the political
condition of the Gold Coast since the exchange of
territory between the English and Dutch Governments, which came into force on the 1st January,
1868, free from all official reticence ; and I hope

that it will enable you, who have shown so much good-will towards the proper government of the West African Settlements, to form a correct idea of our position, so that you may encourage and support any measure that will place the Gold Coast inhabitants in a more prosperous and peaceable state.

In December, 1867, a few days before the actual transfer of territory took place, the Administrator of Her Majesty's Forts and Settlements of the Gold Coast issued a proclamation, setting forth the convention between the Dutch and English Governments relative to the exchange of territory, and the boundary agreed to by the two respective Governments. At the same time a friendly letter was written to the kings and chiefs of the English Protectorate who were about to be transferred, *nolens volens*, informing them that, in order to facilitate trade and civilization, the hitherto Protectorate would be abandoned, that they would be handed over to the Government of the King of the Netherlands, trusting at the same time that their relations with them would be as satisfactory as those they had hitherto maintained with Great Britain.

The principal Dutch town to be transferred was

Dutch Accra ; and accordingly, on the 3rd January, 1868, His Excellency Major Blackhall, Governor-General of the West African Settlements, arrived at British Accra, with the Administrator of the Gold Coast ; on the 4th, the Dutch Governor, from St. George d'Elmina, anchored in the roads ; and at four .p.m. of the same day the Dutch flag was lowered in Fort Greeve Cœur, and the English flag hoisted in its stead, with much ceremony, and under double salutes from the English and Dutch ships of war and from the forts. All the Dutch towns, the most important of which are Appam, Cromantine, and Moree, surrendered to the British authorities without the slightest opposition.

But a different tale must be told of the transfer of the most important district under British protection to the Dutch rule. These people formed nearly one half of the whole population of the Gold Coast, who had always been true and loyal to Her Britannic Majesty's Government, and who were determined, should the English Government refuse to concede to them their former protection, *never to become Dutch*. They therefore drew up a humble petition against the transfer, praying that the British Government would not desert them. The

chiefs of the important districts of Wassaw and
Denkera would not accept either the proclamation,
treaty, or convention. The towns on the sea-coast
were compelled to tolerate the Dutch rule, except
the Commendahs. These people, forming a small
but determined race of men, situated within a few
miles of the town of Elmina, capital of the Dutch
Gold Coast, refused peremptorily to have the
English flag lowered and the Dutch flag hoisted
in its stead. This affront was not by any means
savoury to the Dutch, who immediately bombarded
the town, landed 180 men from their man-of-war,
" Metalen Kruis," set fire to the houses, destroyed
the canoes, killed many of the inhabitants, and
forced the rest to take refuge in the bush.

The bombardment of Commendah acted as an
electric shock throughout the Protectorate ; the
subdued resistance of all the Fantee chiefs now
culminated in armed opposition ; the whole of
the Fantee race flew to arms ; all the kings and
chiefs of the most important provinces of Wassaw,
Denkera, Assin, Fantee, Goomoor, Akenfee,
Anamaboe, and Winnebah, repaired with the King
of Mankessim to their ancient religious city,
Mankessim, where, after a council of war, they

decided to resist by fire and sword the occupation by the Dutch of towns formerly under English protection..

They employed a figurative saying to express the wrong they suffered from the British Government by the transfer. Regarding that Government as their father and protector, and their different tribes as the offspring of that Government, they maintained that the father had no right to make (enslave) them over to another master; and as they were brought up from their youth under the British flag, they were determined not to have themselves handed over to the Dutch authorities.

The inhabitants of Dixcove and British Ahanta, being under the guns of Dixcove Fort, were obliged to submit for a time to their fate, as they were unable to make any open resistance to the Dutch rule; but the people of Wassaw and Denkera, which are situate in the interior, entirely refused to become Dutch. Appolonia, which consists of two districts—viz., Attawaboe and Bainyee, governed by separate kings, formerly under British protection, were divided; the Bainyeans refused to accept the Dutch flag, and the chief town on the sea-coast was consequently bombarded, and the natives retired to the bush towns. They sent to the English Governor at Cape Coast, whom they had always recognized as their chief, for munitions of war to fight against the Dutch, and, being refused, they applied to the Fantee chiefs, who supplied them with powder and lead bar, and several ounces of gold dust. The Attawaboes, being near to the Dutch settlement of Oxeim, quietly accepted their flag.

Thus it is that the transfer of territory, which the British Government thought would have led to the peace and quietude of the Gold Coast Settlement, placed it, from the very commencement, in a state of internal commotion worse than it ever had been in before.

I have the honour to be, Sir,

Your most obedient Servant,

J. A. B. HORTON, M.D.

LETTER No. II.*

TO THE RIGHT HON. EDWARD CARDWELL, HER
MAJESTY'S SECRETARY OF STATE FOR WAR.

CAPE COAST CASTLE,
12th September, 1869.

MY DEAR SIR,

Although the Fantees are akin to
the Elminas under Dutch rule by consanguinity
and by right of nationality—the language of the
latter being only a kind of provincialism of the
former—the Fantees have, from time immemorial,
regarded them as treacherous and not to be de-
pended on ; consequently there has always been a
degree of coldness between the nations.

The Fantees form a compact race, extending
from Wassaw to Winnebah, and include many most
important districts in that tract of land to which
political as well as descriptive writers have applied
the noma—*Protected Territory of the Gold Coast;*
whilst the Elminas, or even the Dutch, own an
extent of country in all scarcely as large as the
province of Wassaw.

---

* Replies, dated 25th November, from Mr. Cardwell (private) and
from Earl Granville.

The Dutch Government on the Gold Coast is an ally to the King of Ashantee—a powerful African potentate, situated behind the Fantee territory, and who has always been the implacable enemy of the Fantees. In years gone by this warlike nation commenced a war of extermination of the whole of that race. Their skilful generals and warlike hordes poured like a swarm of bees from the various provinces of Ashantee (Asanti) into every district of Fantee, paralyzed their efforts towards united action, and produced alarm and consternation wherever they went. In a few pitched battles, where, after several stubborn engagements, ending sometimes in doubtful results, the Ashantees ultimately became victorious, many of the Fantees were laid *hors de combat,* their homes were desolated, their women and children, and those men who had escaped the awful guillotine or the slugs, were carried away captives and sold as slaves. In fact, they invariably signalized their triumph over the Fantees by the most sanguinary sacrifice of hecatombs of captives.

The Ashantees, animated by the most ferocious spirit, would have carried, unchecked, this work of extermination to its fullest extent, had not a stronger and a more valiant arm appeared in the field of battle; and, by the aid of the Congreve rockets, which fell with bloody effect amidst their ranks, a halt was put to their victorious march; and the massacre of Doodoowah by English cannonading sent them flying, helter-skelter, again to their homes; and, by the peace then concluded, the land had rest for several years.

It must, therefore, be conceded that the Fantees, not being British subjects, were perfectly justified in refusing to recognize a treaty or convention which would give to their enemy so much power over them. For the former military roads of the Ashantees in the western district of Fantee were situated in Denkera and Wassaw; but since those provinces threw aside their allegiance to Ashantee and became British, or rather submitted themselves to be under British protection, these roads had been closed against them. The King of Ashantee was ready, even anxiously waiting, the bidding of the Dutch Governor, to send down his military force to his assistance, so as to commence again their long-cherished and favourite " war-whoop " on Fantee; and, as these last had been distinctly informed that their former protector—the British Government—

would have nothing to do with their wars, they considered it their place to disown any arrangement made between the English and Dutch Governments that would place their whole race in jeopardy, and prostrate it before Ashantee. No sooner, therefore, had the Fantee Kings found that the treaty or convention was a *fait accompli*, than they, in solemn conclave, entered into alliance, offensive and defensive, with the Kings of Denkera and Wassaw to oppose the Dutch rule, and to form a confederation amongst themselves for mutual support.

The convention was also objectionable to the inhabitants principally of Cape Coast, because most of their important villages and plantations were transferred to the Dutch rule along with other places, such as Mamfoon, Footoo, Esiachen, &c., so that they would be obliged to submit to Dutch imposts whilst resident at Cape Coast.

This convention brought to life a most important combination on the Gold Coast, which is but the commencement of an independent self-government or confederation of all the provinces in the former Protectorate. In the House of Commons Committee of 1865, the third resolution emphatically stated that

the policy of the Government on the West African
Settlements should now be to encourage in the
natives the exercise of those qualities which may
render it possible for that Government more and
more to transfer to the natives the administration
of all the governments, except perhaps one.   But,
from the steps taken on the Coast by some officials
in high places in respect to progressive development
of natives, as well as from the treatment received
by native chiefs, especially on the Gold Coast,
diametrically opposed to the spirit and letter of
that resolution, every one on the Coast begins to
doubt the sincerity of the statement, and to consider
it as a myth and a delusion, which, consequently, deserves to be placed in the same limbo as many other
good proposals about Africa once rampant but now
entirely defunct.   And I, myself, Sir, should have
been carried away by the popular belief, had I not
become acquainted with the contents of a recent
dispatch of Earl Granville, the present liberal Secretary of State for the Colonies, to his Excellency
the Governor-General of the West African Settlements, wherein he recommended that the natives
should, as much as possible, be brought to know the
intricacies of the civil government of the Coast, with

the ultimate view of placing them in responsible governmental position.

The Fantee Confederation sprang into existence soon after the promulgation of the treaty and actual transfer of territory between the Dutch and English rule on the Gold Coast. It is composed of all the Kings of Fantee who had, up to January 1, 1868, been under the British flag. The object, as has been detailed to me, is couched in two brief but pregnant phrases—viz.: 1st, To advance the interest of the whole of the Fantee nation ; and, 2ndly, to combine for offence and defence in time of war.

At present this Confederation is in an embryonic state, without any code of law which a civilized government might consider as binding, or necessary for the proper working of the Confederation ; the people are, as it were, feeling their way cautiously in the mystic labyrinth of constitutional self-government.

The King of Abrah, or Abacrampa, who from time immemorial has been regarded as the leader of the Fantee nation, without whose first move into the field the inhabitants would not leave their homes, feels jealous that King Edoo, of Mankessim, should now arrogate to himself the leadership of the

Confederation, and would not recognize him as
such ; so that there is at present a slight coldness
between the two potentates. There is, therefore,
no real president to the Confederation ; but a chief
magistrate, who is also the treasurer, and a secretary have been appointed, both chosen from the
intelligent and educated portion of the population,
and of known character and influence.

Ever since the Ashantee expedition of 1864,
which ended in results not by any means praiseworthy to the protecting power, the natives of this
Coast have been repeatedly told that they must
defend their own firesides, and that the British Government would give them no assistance in case
they were to be attacked in the interior, except,
perhaps, by supplying them with munitions of war.
The appeal to all the inhabitants to unite in forming
a self-government, and the necessity for making
such appeal, is most graphically described in the
following address to the Fantee nation, written by
one of them : " On the 18th July of the current
year, after certain correspondence had passed between them, his Excellency the Administrator, H.
T. Ussher, addressed a letter to the presidents and
other chiefs of Fantee, at Mankessim, in which, after

censuring the conduct of the said presidents and chiefs, and after going into various circumstances connected with the Elmina war, his Excellency proceeds to state, ' Your conduct has been such that I can no longer have any relation with you ;' and ' as you voluntarily throw off your allegiance, you must not be surprised that I accept your act, and treat you, until you come to your senses, as apart from Great Britain;' further, that ' in case of war with the Ashantees, as you will have provoked it, you will bear the brunt thereof without help from Government.' Such being the facts, the Ashantees having already invaded the territories of our friends and allies (the Wassaws and Denkeras), the British Government having disowned us, and informed us that we are not to expect any assistance from it in case of an Ashantee invasion—our wisest and safest policy lies in our adopting, without delay, some measures for our self-government, and our self-defence."

I have the honour to be, Sir,

Your most obedient Servant,

J. A. B. HORTON, M.D.

LETTER No. III.*

TO THE RIGHT HON. EDWARD CARDWELL, HER
MAJESTY'S SECRETARY OF STATE FOR WAR.

> CAPE COAST CASTLE,
> 12*th October*, 1869.

MY DEAR SIR,

Hitherto I have considered the important combination which has been formed between
the various kings of Fantee, who occupy the western
district of the Gold Coast ; but the eastern district,
composed entirely of a different nationality, and
separated from Fantee by a natural boundary, took
no part whatever in this combination. Unlike the
kings in the interior of the western districts, the
kings in the interior of the eastern district have
from time immemorial regarded the principal king on
the sea-coast town as their head, so that any command
or order issued by him receives immediate obedience.
Circumstances which have sprung up since the unsettled state of the country have compelled the
educated natives, in conjunction with the kings on
the sea coast—viz., of James Town, Old Dutch

---

* Reply, dated 2nd December, from Earl Granville.

Accra, and Christiansborg—to form a close political combination, whose first object is to bring to a speedy termination the wars and disturbances which have nearly ruined Accra. It was stipulated at a general meeting held on the evening of the 13th August last, by the educated natives, which was joyfully assented to by the kings and chiefs—" That, considering the immense stake the educated natives hold in the country, and the interest they therefore have in the preservation of peace and order therein ; and considering further that the kings themselves have acknowledged their utter want of power to grapple with the political condition of the country, *Resolved*—That in future it shall not be competent for the kings of themselves to moot any question affecting the object set forth above, either by themselves personally or by communication with the Government, without first consulting with the body of educated natives and receiving their consent."

A managing committee, consisting of six gentlemen of education, was appointed, having W. Lutterodt, Esq., as the president, to act in conjunction with the kings in conducting the affairs of the country generally. They have subscribed handsomely towards buying munitions of war, and have

tendered very wholesome suggestions to the officer
in civil command of the district with reference to
the present political crisis of the country.*

---

* The following is a letter addressed by Mr. James Bannerman
to me relative to the formation of the Accra Native Confederation :—

" Cape Coast, Sept. 21, 1869.

" MY DEAR DOCTOR,

"Referring to our conversation of the other evening
relative to the present political aspect of affairs in the eastern
districts of the Gold Coast generally, but Accra in particular, I
rejoice to have it in my power to inform you that the political condition of Accra possesses now, although only in the germ, I may
say, such elements of good, that, properly and sincerely fostered by
the educated natives, will, I feel sure, eventually be the source of
lasting advantage to our part of the country. There has very
recently been formed a close political combination between the
educated natives of Accra and the kings of Jamestown, old Dutch
Accra, and Christiansborg, these three chiefs representing the tribes
inhabiting the sea-board and the interior of the eastern districts,
which combination, formed on a firm and apparently durable basis,
appears to me to be the germ of that form of government (Re-
publican) which you have advocated in your book on Western
Africa. I will endeavour to explain as concisely as possible, but
imperfectly, how this new, important move, originated, and by what
means it was accomplished. The result of the Awoonah expedition
in 1866 forcibly proved to the educated natives of Accra that under
similar circumstances in the future, if they should not be prepared
and determined to rely on their own resources, it was impossible
that they could hope to meet with success in any future expeditions
they might undertake. It is true that for the Awoonah expedition
Colonel Conran distributed to Kings Cogoe and Dowoonah 1,200
muskets for the use of 8,000 men, with a number of kegs of ball
cartridge, the use of which they did not properly understand, and

Let us now turn to the western, or Fantee district, and we shall find that soon after the bombardment of Commendah by the Dutch man-of-war, the

---

the European and native traders also subscribed to a fund for the chiefs to purchase ammunition (the chiefs being really without the means to do anything for themselves); but this assistance in munitions of war was ultimately found to be ridiculously inadequate for carrying out an expedition of that kind as had been planned by Col. Conran; and it was only got through the noble personal efforts of poor Irvine, who, at great inconvenience and personal loss, ultimately procured sufficient powder and lead for the chiefs. It is true the European and native traders also subscribed to the fund for purchasing this ammunition, but it was in the proportion of 10*l.* to Mr. Irvine's 40*l.* I say, then, this incident in the expedition fully showed us educated natives that the time had come when it was imperatively incumbent on us to rely on ourselves, and ourselves alone, under future similar circumstances, as it was not likely that we should always possess European friends of the same calibre as Mr. Irvine, who had so thoroughly identified himself with the real interests of the country; nor ought we expect from the local government more than a little substantial aid at a time. On our return from the expedition, therefore, the question was mooted amongst us whether some means should not be devised amongst the educated natives alone to guard ourselves against future similar emergencies. In mentioning, however, one day, in conversation with the late Mr. Irvine, our intention in reference to this movement,-my friend appeared and expressed himself really so hurt at the very idea of being severed from any future opportunity of joining the natives in matters affecting the country whose real interests he had always endeavoured faithfully to advance, that it was determined to try other modes of proceeding. Mr. Irvine's lamented death removed the only obstacle for our carrying out our proposed plan of combination amongst ourselves. Since the expedition to

Commendahs caught and killed a native of Elmina, a
Dutch Fantee, and sent his jaw-bone to the Fantee
kings, who were then assembled at Mankessim for

Awoonah other important considerations have tended to strengthen
the determination formed by the educated natives to put their
shoulders to the wheel for the public good. The most important of
these considerations is the patent and admitted fact of the inability
(from sheer want of means, in men or money) of the chiefs to
exercise the same kind of government over their people on the sea-
board as their more wealthy brethren of the western district of the
Gold Coast. (I say as regards controlling their subjects on the
sea-coast; as far as the chiefs in the interior are concerned, the
chiefs of Accra, by combined action in council in all matters affecting
the whole eastern districts, can issue commands through King
Tackee to, and those orders are obeyed by, the other chiefs in the
interior.) The kings of Accra, unlike the Fantees, have very few,
if any, personal followers, and next to nothing of—what is equal to
any amount of slaves—the sinews of war. The educated natives
alone can aid the kings with followers in times of war, the men or
slaves whom they possess having descended to them from their
fathers, who purchased, or rather redeemed, their (the people's)
ancestors when about to be shipped off the coast in the ancient dark
days of the slave-trade. These men have proved under their
masters of some service to the Government on various occasions in
times past, from 1822 to 1863. I merely mention this in order to
point out to you plainly the ruling causes which have influenced us,
at this juncture of political affairs, to presume to differ so diametrically in opinion from that which seems to have been formed
and adhered to by his Excellency the Acting Administrator, who
thinks the kings quite capable of taking matters entirely into their
own hands whether in peace or in war. In March last, when the
alliance between the Aquamboes and Ashantees assumed a threatening aspect towards the eastern districts, and hostilities had actually

solemn deliberation on the events that had taken place. This organ was forwarded as a symbol that they had commenced hostilities against the Dutch.

---

commenced between these two tribes and the Krepees, who are closely allied to the Accras, Mr. Simpson visited Accra for the purpose of urging the kings to make a move towards the seat of war, and for that purpose he required them to furnish 2,000 men, with a captain in command, to hasten to the assistance of the Akim Chief Domprey, who, heading the Krepees, was fighting single-handed and gallantly resisting the combined forces of Ashantee, Aquamboe, and Awoonah; his Excellency promising to supply them with ammunition as soon as they commenced to move. The kings readily, of course, consented to do what the Governor required, and engaged to send forward the 2,000 men in two weeks. His Excellency then, much satisfied with this promise, and believing in the ability of the kings to perform it, gave them an order on the public chest for 100*l.* in order to prepare the proposed expedition. Their majesties received the cash from the commandant, and quietly shared it amongst themselves. A few weeks afterwards Lutterodt, Cleland, myself, and others of the educated natives, who were quietly watching the course of events, one day met Kings Tackee and Cogoe, and asked them when their contingent of 2,000 men would move to the seat of war? They replied, very sheepishly, that they did not know, and they thought they would ultimately have to seek assistance from us. Matters remained in this unsatisfactory state until the melancholy death of poor Irvine occurred, and then was aroused again in greater force than ever the feelings amongst the educated natives that *something must be done amongst ourselves* to assist the chiefs in restoring order to the country by finding means to check the invasion of the territory by the Ashantees. Mr. Simpson, after several futile attempts to persuade the kings to keep their promise of moving 2,000 men to the seat of war to assist Domprey, gave up the thankless task in disgust and despair. Had

A council of war was immediately assembled,
consisting of the following kings, with their chiefs
and their principal men—viz., Edoo of Mankessim,

Mr. Simpson taken the trouble to consult *one* educated native of
respectability in this matter, he would have saved himself much
trouble and ridicule, and the Government some expense. On the
12th August Mr. William Lutterodt, residing at old Dutch Accra,
the acknowledged head of the educated natives of Accra, invited to
a meeting at his house all the educated natives, numbering about
sixty respectable persons, to hear what the kings had decided on
doing in respect of the prosecution of the war. Nothing whatever
resulted from this meeting as regards the intentions held by the
kings, who plainly declared they were powerless without us. Immediately after the meeting broke up, invitations were issued to
thirty of the principal educated natives to meet at my house on the
following evening (the 13th), and accordingly on the evening of the
13th we met together (Mr. Bartels having been requested to be
present). I cannot now give you in detail all that occurred;
suffice it to say that, after the attention of the meeting had been
forcibly drawn by seven or eight prominent speakers to the present
deplorable state of the country, the inability of the Government to
do more than give a little pecuniary aid alone under the circumstances, and the acknowledged utter inability of the kings to *do anything* unaided by us, it was, after a further short discussion amongst
the other persons at the meeting, unanimously resolved that an
association of the educated natives should at once be formed for
the following purposes : That, considering the immense stake the
educated natives hold in the country, and the interest they therefore
have in the preservation of peace and order therein, and considering
further that the kings themselves have acknowledged their utter
want of power to compass the objects for which this meeting has
been convened, that in future it shall not be competent to the kings
of themselves to moot any questions affecting the objects set forth

Otoo of Abrah, Akinney of Akumfie, Autable of Goomoor, Ammonoo of Anamaboe, and Meekor of Ajimakoo, besides other kings of lesser note.   Each

---

above, either by themselves or by communication with the Government, without first consulting with the body of educated natives and receiving their consent.   This is the pith and substance of the resolution arrived at on the evening of the 13th August.   Before the meeting, however, broke up, six of the educated natives present were elected by the meeting to act as a managing committee in the affairs of the country generally in conjunction with the kings, and this committee was requested to draw up certain rules for the guidance of themselves and the kings, no affairs of general interest, however, to be discussed or carried out without the presence or the consent of the whole body of educated natives.   This committee is composed of W. Lutterodt (president), L. Hope, Geo. Cleland, J. E. Richter, W. Addor, and myself.   On the 14th August the committee met the kings of Accra, and laid before them the resolution which had been arrived at at the meeting the previous evening.   The kings at once joyfully consented to the propositions laid before them, and promised faithfully for the future to act in *all* matters, whether in peace or for foreign war, in conjunction and harmony with the educated natives, and to be guided alone by their advice through their president. Immediately after this the committee communicated to Captain Russell, the late Commandant of Accra, the results of the recent meeting ; and at a subsequent interview with him, at his request, that officer heard with considerable attention several suggestions offered by the committee in reference to the present political crisis of the eastern district.   Captain Russell, while perfectly coinciding with the opinions expressed by the committee, regretted his inability to do anything for them, his term of office having that day expired, but he promised to make known our suggestions to his successor, Captain Lees, who, he had no doubt, would forward them to the proper quarter, and he would recommend him to do so.   At a

one took their great or fetish oath that they would
stand or fall by the tribes who had been recently
transferred, fight their battles, and resist step by
step any encroachment of the Dutch. And they
agreed that preparations should be made to face
the Dutch in their own territory, and attempt, if
possible, to drive them into the sea, and hand over
the Dutch territory to the English Government.
Their war-cry was that the Dutch Fantee should
be conquered, and be made *majestem populi Anglici
comiter conservanto*—*i.e.*, loyally to acknowledge the
supremacy of the English people.

---

subsequent date, at the request of Captain Lees, the committee and
the kings met Captain Lees, who also expressed his concurrence in
our views generally, but also expressed his inability to assist us
unauthorized by the Governor, but he gave us his earnest assurance
of all the aid he could possibly afford us. Thus has been at last
formed this important combination, which necessarily is at present
circumscribed in its objects and actions, which appear now to be to
bring to a speedy close the wars and disturbances which have well
nigh brought Accra to ruin. and for this purpose the educated
natives have subscribed out of their own pockets 300*l.* for ammunition for the chiefs; and it is to be hoped that the Government and
the European merchants will not be left at a distance by the educated
natives in this public subscription for the benefit of the whole community. So soon as success shall have crowned the efforts now
being made to bring this war to a speedy issue, it will be the duty
of the managing committee to turn their efforts earnestly to the
improvement of their country in the arts of peace and civilization,

A few days after the atrocious conduct of the Commendahs, the Elminas, by way of retaliation, fell unexpectedly on two families, to the number of twelve persons, who had for years resided in one of their villages as peaceful farmers, mortally wounded some of them, and marched the rest as prisoners through the town of Elmina, where they were rescued by the Dutch authorities. The report of these audacious proceedings produced consternation in the ranks of the Fantee kings. Otoo of Abrah, the vanguard of the Fantee army, was ordered to march immediately to Effatoo with his men, where he was

---

and I doubt not that, with God's help, we shall soon learn practically the art of self-government. This very imperfect sketch, my dear Doctor, will give you but a very slight inkling of the aims and objects of our new but important movement. I see in the future as the result of this combination the " foundation of a good, useful, native self-government, profitable both to the English Government and the native population ; " for the kings left to themselves " the whole fabric of their Government, rotten at the base, *has* fallen to the ground." A new *régime has* been established, which, supported (not pooh-poohed) by the Government, will in time attain inestimable results.

Yours faithfully, my dear Doctor,

J. BANNERMAN.

Dr. Horton, M.D.

P.S.—The Awoonahs, who signed the treaty with Sir Arthur Kennedy, and the Aquamboes, who all signed the same treaty with Mr. Simpson, are now at open war with the allies of the Accras.

soon joined by Quachiframe, King of Denkera. The combined forces now moved on to Semue, and were there joined by King Edoo and his followers. All the different kings now rapidly arrived in camp, and took their disposition around Elmina.

Whilst these movements were going on in the interior, the Administrator of the Gold Coast issued a proclamation suspending indefinitely the sale of powder, lead bars, guns, fire-arms, and all other arms and munitions of war, from the Sweet River to the River Volta ; and making parties infringing the same liable to heavy penalties, in addition to the confiscation and seizure of the goods so sold. The inhabitants of Cape Coast and district were warned against meddling with the interior disturbances, and were impressed with the necessity of remaining perfectly neutral.

On the 28th February, 1868, the Administrator, H. T. Ussher, Esq., wrote to King Amfoo Otoo of Abrah, informing him that it had come to his knowledge that he, in common with the Fantee chiefs, had dispatched a large force of armed men to attack the Dutch at Commendah, and to aid the rebellious people of that place, requesting to know the truth of the intelligence, and also warning them not to compel him to use extreme measures against them, who are dependents of England.

King Otoo, in reply to the Administrator's letter, acknowledged the truth of the report, but alleged as an excuse that the Elmina people, who are under the Dutch flag, had sent three companies to assist the Dutch Government to destroy the Commendahs. The kings stated that it was beyond their comprehension how the people of Commendah, who are not slaves of either Government, could be bartered off in the transfer, and, when they refuse to go under the Dutch flag, their town should be bombarded, and the people sent adrift into the forest. The kings, whilst acknowledging their loyalty to the British Government, quietly reminded the Administrator that the land on which the neglected river fort of Commendah now stands is the property of the people, and that they received ground-rent for it when the African Company governed this coast.

Whilst negotiations were going on between the Administrator and the Fantee kings, and whilst the Fantee armed forces were increasing around Elmina, reports of musketry were heard by the Cape Coast people in the interior on the 4th April, 1868. It appears that the Elminas, to the number of some 500 armed men (report says 2,000), taking advantage of the unprotected condition of the left of the Fantee force, suddenly attacked a village belonging to Cape Coast containing from 150 to 200 inhabitants, killed four of them and made prisoners of a few, and the rest escaped unhurt. This was a signal for the inhabitants of Cape Coast, who, being under the guns of the Castle and of Fort William, were hesitating (after receiving positive orders from the Administrator not to join the chiefs in the interior) what steps they should take. They now flew to arms and marched into the field, amidst the hurrahs of their women and children, with their " Headman " Attah as their leader, despite the remonstrances of the chief of the Executive Government.

Foiled in his attempt of preventing the Cape Coast people from joining the Fantee army encamped near Elmina, the Administrator issued a proclamation wherein he accused Chief Quassie Attah of a breach of his oath of allegiance, in consequence of which he was to be considered as " an outlaw, and deprived of his office and dignity," his property forfeited and confiscated to the Crown. It was further decreed—which decree was carried out to the letter—that the house of Quassie Attah should be pulled down and demolished, as a warning to all seditious people at Cape Coast.

Whilst these proceedings were going on at Cape Coast, the forces of that place had arrived at Abinah, the village which the Elminas had attacked and burnt ; they immediately advanced, opened fire on and drove back the Elminas. The Fantee force had now amounted to 15,000 fighting men (report says 30,000), and were thus disposed around Elmina :—

On *the left*, at the village of Abinah—the forces of Cape Coast, great and small Cromantine, Moree (lately transferred from the Dutch to the English), and a portion of Goomoor.

On *the centre*, encamped at Frampoon, were the forces of Abrah, Ajimacoo, Ayen, and Mankessim.

On *the right* were the forces of Denkera, Anamaboe, Akumfie, and Cheefall. The Commendahs were stationed on the extreme right.

Whilst the Fantee army was thus disposing itself in preparation for an attack, the Administrator dispatched Mr. T. B. Freeman to the camp to endeavour to prevent the hostile intention of the kings and chiefs, and if possible bring about ami-

cable arrangements between the Fantees and the
Dutch ; but his efforts were unsuccessful at first. A
council of war was assembled on Saturday, the 23rd
May, to determine the time and mode of attack. It
was agreed that on Thursday following, early in the
morning, the Commendahs on the extreme right
should commence the fight, and a general attack
should be made on the lines of the Elminas, the
left to force in their right, and the centre to decide
the fate of the day. This decision was to be kept
as private as possible.

But the Elminas were amongst those to whom,
in the language of the Grecian bards, " the gods are
willing to reveal themselves."

οὐ γάρ πω πάντεσσι Θεοὶ φαύνονται ἐναργεῖς.—ΟΔΥΣ. Π, v. 161.

There was a spy unrecognized in the camp in
the person of a Fantee by birth, but who had
resided for many years and found intimate connexions in Elmina. He communicated the decision
to the Elmina chiefs, who, with the Dutch regular
troops, made a vigorous attack on the right of the
Fantee forces early on Tuesday morning, the 26th
May. The Cape Coast force, although taken by
surprise, met them resolutely, and drove them back.

The Elminas having now commenced the fight,

whilst the left of the Fantee force was continuing the engagement, the centre, consisting of Ayen, a part of Abrah, and Mankessim, advanced and attacked the centre of the Elmina force ; at the same time the Anamaboes and others on the right pressed them hard on the left. A general engagement ensued, the Elminas and Dutch troops were driven in on all sides into the town.   The victorious army pursued them rapidly to the outskirts of the town, when a murderous fire was opened by the heavy ordnance of the Dutch from Fort St. Jago, which staggered them for a moment.   The Dutch camps were set on fire ; several of their needle rifles and small arms captured ; attempts were made to set the town on fire without avail.   At 2.30 P.M. the left and centre ceased pursuit, and at 3 P.M the right also ceased.   The Elminas or Dutch made no attempt to renew the attack, and it was decided by the Fantees to commence operations against them the next day.

In this engagement the greater part of the Fantee force took no part. The King of Abrah, either from jealousy or from the influence of the British envoy in the camp, withheld most of his men.   The Commendahs on the extreme right, who

were to commence the fight on Thursday, knew
nothing of what was going on, but they were now
ordered to join. Whilst preparations were being
made for the work of the morrow, the British envoy
redoubled his efforts for the maintenance of peace,
and prevailed on the Fantee kings, since, as he
argued, they had avenged the insult to their honour,
to place the dispute between the Elminas and
themselves in the hands of the Administrator for
adjustment. The next day after the engagement,
whilst most of the men were preparing to renew
the attack, a report, which proved too true, was
circulated, that the King of Abrah with his people
had removed their encamping ground ten miles
from the seat of war. Towards evening, their
example was followed by nearly three-fourths of
the army, and the Elmina war terminated with the
retreat of the whole of the Fantee force the next
day.

A commission, consisting of W. H. Simpson,
Esq., collector of customs, T. B. Freeman, Esq,
envoy extraordinary, and W. Dawson, Esq., secretary of the Fantee kings and chiefs, were dispatched by the Administrator on board H.M.
Ship " Pandora " to Elmina, to negotiate with

the Dutch Governor and the kings and chiefs of Elmina terms of peace, the substance of which was :—

1. That hostilities between the two parties should cease indefinitely.

2. That the alliance between the Elminas and and Ashantees be suspended for six months.

3. That the Elminas be allowed free intercourse with and through every part of the Fantee District.

This treaty was to be prepared on parchment, and signed by the kings and chiefs of Fantee and Elmina, or their representatives, at the Sweet River which divides the two territories. The Fantee kings repudiated *in toto* the provisions of the treaty and refused to have anything to do with the proceeding, unless the Elminas should make their alliance with Ashantee null and void, and unite with them, offensive and defensive, against Ashantee. The Elminas on their part preferred retaining their alliance with the latter power; and since that time Elmina has been besieged on the land side— the inhabitants have been and still are in a state of semi-starvation. Now and then sorties are made by one or other of the hostile people; an unprotected village becomes the object of their fury; a

few of the inhabitants are perhaps taken captives,
their heads and hands cut off, placed in a basin or
calabash, and paraded round the town amidst yells
of barbaric triumph.

I have the honour to be, Sir,

Your most obedient Servant,

J. A. B. HORTON, M.D.

LETTER No. IV.*

TO THE RIGHT HON. EARL GRANVILLE, K.G., D.C.L., SECRETARY OF STATE FOR THE COLONIES.

CAPE COAST CASTLE,
12th November, 1869.

MY LORD,

In three successive letters, dated respectively the 12th August, 12th September, and 12th October last, which I had the honour to address to the Right Hon. Edward Cardwell, late Secretary of State for the Colonies, at present Her Majesty's Secretary of State for War, I endeavoured to point out as clearly as possible the political state of the Gold Coast territory, from the time that the treaty of exchange of territory between the English and Dutch Governments became an accomplished fact, down to the termination of the Elmina war. In a letter, dated the 11th September last, the Right Hon. the Secretary of State for War, in reply to my letter of the 12th August, informed me that as he " has no longer any immediate connexion with the subject " treated of, he has forwarded my letter to your lordship, " to

---

* Reply dated 29th December.

whom any further letters on the subject had better be addressed."

It will be necessary for me, at this state of the subject, to take a retrospective glance at the political atmosphere of the whole Gold Coast territory just before the ratification of the treaty, and which in fact gave rise to the negotiation on the subject between the Courts of St. James's and the Hague.

Up to the end of 1862, when Richard Pine, Esq., landed here as Governor of Her Majesty's Forts and Settlements on the Gold Coast, the country was in the most prosperous state; the blessings of peace had been felt and enjoyed for many years; all the kings and chiefs in the interior were in perfect amity and concord with one another; the Ashantees were in the most friendly relations with Fantees and the British authorities; trade was in the most flourishing condition; bands of Ashantee merchants poured daily from the interior into the coast towns, loaded with gold dust, ivory, and other marketable articles, which they exchanged for European goods and munitions of war. Even in Ashantidom, their interior wars had been settled satisfactorily, and they had celebrated a gala day in commemoration of their victories. The Ashantees, who are the life blood of

the Gold Coast commerce, were now (being freed
from internal commotions) bent on carrying on an
extensive trade with the sea-coast towns. The Crobboes in the eastern district, through the influence
of Governor Pine, were gladly paying their debt.
There was a sort of happy lull in the political condition of the whole country, when, about the
beginning of the year 1863, a misunderstanding
arose between the British authorities and the King
of Ashantee, which at first threatened the peace of
the Protectorate, and which ultimately culminated
in open hostilities between the two Governments.

The affair appeared at first to be very easy of
amicable arrangement. It was reported to the King
of Ashantee that one of his lieutenants or chiefs,
Quacoo Gamin by name, had, contrary to the laws
of the country, found and appropriated to his own
use a quantity of gold nuggets. The King sum-
moned him to appear in person at his Court in
Coomassie (the capital) on a certain day. Gamin
received the summons and promised to appear at the
day and hour appointed ; but being apprehensive of
danger, he quietly fled with 80 of his adherents, subjects of Ashantee, to the British protected territory
of Denkera. Quacoo Duah, King of Ashantee, one

of the most peaceful rulers that has ever sat on the throne, sent a princely ambassador, accompanied by a numerous and richly-dressed retinue, to Her Majesty's representative, to give the necessary information of the case and demand the extradition of the runaways. At a meeting held at the Palaver Hall, in the Castle of Cape Coast, in which were assembled the Governor and Council, both executive and legislative, the Commodore of the station, the officer commanding the troops, the principal merchants (European and native), and the kings and chiefs principally of Cape Coast and its environs, the whole affair was warmly discussed. The case of the King of Ashantee was set forth in a speech by his war-axe bearer, which was remarkable for its fluency, rhetorical power, and argumentative clearness. There was a division amongst the members. Many of the merchants, with Commodore Wilmot, strongly urged the claim of the King of Ashantee, and recommended that Gamin should be delivered up ; whilst the chiefs of Cape Coast, who had been bribed by Gamin and some of the merchants, were of a contrary opinion. Commodore Wilmot endeavoured to influence them,. by showing them how prosperous the country then was and the evils of war, and clearly pointed out that, if they went to war with Ashantee, it would take fifty years to bring the country back to its then condition ; but, *quot homines tot sententiæ*, the voice of the multitude prevailed, and Gamin was quietly allowed to remain in the Protectorate. War was declared by the King of Ashantee, who made extensive preparations to invade the Gold Coast territory.

Viewing the state of affairs at this peculiar crisis of the country, an impartial witness cannot help justifying both parties for the part they played in it—viz., Governor Pine in retaining Gamin, and the King of Ashantee in immediately declaring war ; but the balance of justification rests with the King of Ashantee, and this I shall prove by my observations made at the time.*

Governor Pine was justified, because, according to the British law, a refugee who cannot be proved to have committed any crime, and who claims protection from our Government, cannot legally be delivered up to a tyrant or a despotic government. It is well known that the lives of the refugees, if they had been delivered up, would have been sacri-

---

* African Times, 1863—Page 138.

ficed.   No sooner would they have crossed the
frontier, than their heads would have been taken off
and sent to the King of Ashantee at Coomassie ;
and Gamin requested that his head should rather
be cut off at the Castle-gate, than that he should be
delivered to the king.

The King of Ashantee was justified in declaring
war, because—First, the very throne on which he
sat was in danger.   If he had not acted promptly
in this affair, his people would have branded him as
a coward, and consequently unworthy to occupy the
stool of the long-famed and brave kings of
Ashantee.   Second, if the refugees were allowed to
remain quietly in the Protectorate, without any
demonstration being made regarding them, more important men would also have followed their example,
and sought protection and security in the quiet
rule of the British Government.   Third, before there
was any commencement of actual hostilities between
the two nations, the peaceful traders of the King
of Ashantee were molested by the Fantees in the
interior ; their goods, consisting principally of munitions of war, were seized, and the men themselves
put in irons.   They were, however, released, but no
compensation was given to them.   Fourth, on such

an occasion, the generals and captains of the King
of Ashantee would swear the great oath—viz., that
the king had received an unpardonable insult, and
that they were determined to avenge it.   After this
oath, the king would be powerless to prevent them
from marching an army against his enemies. It will
therefore be seen that war was inevitable, since the
runaways were detained ; and as regards the author
of the war, in defence of the King of Ashantee I
leave Montesquieu to reply to it ; he said, that "the
true author of war is not he who declares it, but he
who renders it necessary."

After collecting a force of about 30,000 men, the
King of Ashantee made three grand divisions of his
army, and placed them under an experienced
general of royal blood—viz., Prince Owoosookorkor
or Osoo Cokkor.   The smallest division, consisting
of about 2,000 men, was sent to the boundary of
Wassaw on the west, with orders to avoid as much
as possible any general engagement with the enemy,
but to keep the Wassaws and Denkeras in check,
and prevent them from joining the Fantee force.
The second division, consisting of about 8,000 men,
descended, after crossing the Praah, on the main-
road towards Cape Coast, and pushed rapidly into

the middle of the country as far as it was safe, avoiding any engagement with superior forces. The third division and main body, under the personal command of Prince Osoo Cokkor, marched on the east of Fantee through Akim, the most powerful and warlike people in the Protectorate, forcing everything before them. This tactic was intended to prevent the Aquamboos and Accras from joining the kings in the eastern portion of Fantee.

Whilst these preparations were being made at Coomassie, the British force, consisting of small detachments of the 2nd and 3rd West India Regiments, and the late Gold Coast Artillery Corps, numbering about 400 men, were distributed in the eastern districts of the Protectorate—at James Town, Accra, Prampram, Quanti-nang, and Kpong—for the express purpose of effecting the early settlement of the long-standing Crobboe fine. His Excellency Richard Pine, Esq., Governor, had personally visited that province, and whilst in that district he received a dispatch, confirming the rumour that three divisions of the Ashantee army had crossed the frontier and descended on British territory. Orders were immediately dispatched to recall the troops from the different outposts.

Fortunately a detachment of the 2nd West India Regiment, from Lagos, arrived at Accra at this opportune moment, on board the transport, in which the other troops were embarked for Cape Coast. Preparations were rapidly pushed forward for taking the field. Most of the natives who were able to bear arms left their towns to form various encampments in opposition to the Ashantee forces. Great difficulty was experienced in obtaining transports for the guns, ammunition, and other stores for the regular troops, so that women and children were employed for that purpose. Captain Wood, R.N., a revenue officer of the Government, received a com mission as major of volunteers, and was ordered to proceed to Mansoo to organize the native force there, which comprises the inhabitants of Assin, Abrah, Denkera, Cape Coast, and Anamboe. The Cape Coast Volunteers were under the command of Captain Hutchinson, merchant; they were composed of the intelligent natives of that place.

Whilst these preparations were being made on our side, a report was received that a severe encounter had taken place in a considerable town of Agoonah, called Essicoomab. The Ashantees descending from Western Akim, whose king, Agiman, and subjects had fallen back as the Ashantees approached, met an army of the Agoonahs and Goomoors, who had posted themselves in the forest and roads to give them battle. The Fantees first opened fire, which was warmly replied to by the Ashantees; and after a severe engagement, which lasted for six hours, in which both armies fought bravely, and many men on both sides were placed *hors de combat*, the Ashantees became masters of the field, and the Fantee force made a rapid retreat to the camp of Ajimacoo. This victory was most important to the Ashantees, not only because it preserved their ancient *prestigé*, but also because, whilst it struck terror to the enemy, it inspired courage amongst themselves. Again, it opened a direct line of communication between their army at Assin and the main body.

The British forces now hastened to the field. 400 regulars and about 70 volunteers, under the command of Major Cochrane, marched, on the 19th April, 1863, from the seaport town of Anamaboe to Mankessim. On their arrival, Captain Brownwell, with 100 men, was detailed to proceed to Winnebah, which was then threatened by a body of the enemy. The troops remained ten days at

Mankessim, which is about twenty-two miles from
Essicoomah, which latter place formed the head-
quarters of Prince Osoo Cokkor, the Ashantee commander-in-chief.   They afterwards marched on to
Bobecoomah, where a large native force (irregulars)
were collected. The Ashantee army, after the battle
of Essicoomah, marched proudly through the province of Akumfie into Goomar, and in the neighbourhood of Bobecoomah rashly advanced to a most
dangerous position, where, if attacked with vigour
and pertinacity, they would have been annihilated.
The British force at Bobecoomah were now for the
first time placed within a very short distance from their
implacable foe. Scouts were sent out, which brought
in positive evidence that the Ashantees were within
a quarter of a mile of the camp.   Some of them
had been wounded by the enemy, many killed, and
others escaped unhurt.   Yet still, with all these
positive proofs before him, the officer commanding
both the British forces and the native irregulars
(20,000 strong) did not, or rather would not, permit
himself to believe them, but issued immediately an
order to the effect that the regular troops, as well as
the greater part of the native troops, should march
on to a small village called Endume, which was

some distance away from the enemy's camp, leaving only 5,000 at Bobecoomah. Some of the regular troops, with a great many of their officers, and the whole of the irregulars who had been told off, arrived the next day at Endume ; the major commanding and staff, with the half of his regulars as body guard, marched in a tangent from Bobecoomah and Endume, and established his head-quarters at Mumford, on the seacoast, twenty miles away from Endume. The officers of the 3rd West India Regiment, who had according to orders proceeded to Endume, were surprised not to find the officer commanding in the camp the next morning. The whole of the force which left Bobecoomah were dispersed in every direction ; some were at Mumford, some at Endume, whilst a detachment found its way to Winnebah.

The Ashantees, flushed with the victory of Essicoomah, were determined now to try their whole force with the combined native and British troops. After driving in the pickets of the allied army, and whilst this crazy manoeuvre was being strategically per·formed, on Wednesday, the 12th May, 1863, at two o'clock, the Ashantees opened fire upon the native army of Bobecoomah, which had been so disgracefully deserted the day before. The battle lasted from two until five p.m., leaving the Ashantees masters of the town, with a large number of men in killed, wounded, and prisoners. The town was razed to the ground ; and had Prince Osoo Cokkor pressed his victorious army further and marched on to Endume, he would have effected an easy victory over the panic-stricken host, which would have retaliated for their losses in Doodoowah, nearly forty years ago. But he was a man of vacillating character, and, although loudly advised by the several princes of the blood who held subordinate positions as commanders of divisions in his army, including two of the King's brothers, several of his sons, and the general's own elder brother, he refused to venture any further.

About this time a reinforcement of 180 men arrived from Sierra Leone and Gambia in H.M. ships "Dart" and "Dover." Forty were sent to Accra, and the rest (140) were ordered to Mansoo, under Captain, now Lieutenant-Colonel Harley, where a large native force had been remaining inactive in camp for more than one month.

Confusion now reigned within the ranks of the allied British and native forces, and nothing could be heard but loud discontent in the mouths of every one. The Ashantees having defeated the allied force in two actions, and having successfully maintained their footing in the most fertile province of the Gold Coast for eighty days, during which time they lived on the produce of the towns and villages, burnt or otherwise destroyed the cereals and other native food, razed to the ground about thirty-four towns and villages, and about double the number of plantations, fell back upon their own resources, or retired on towns bordering on the frontiers of Ashantee on the 24th May, unmolested by an equal number of the allied forces who were watching their movements.

Soon after the action at Bobecoomah, His Excellency R. Pine, under escort of a body of volunteers, organized by and in the pay of Mr., then Captain, William Charles Finlason, of Cape Coast, marched into the field, and pitched his camp at Denkare (Akumfie), a few miles from Ajimacoo, where a large body of native force had congregated. He endeavoured to inspire them with new spirit; and, in consultation with Major Cochrane, it was agreed to make a simultaneous attack on the Ashantee force, which was then at Akim Swadrue. At this

time Prince Osoo Cokkor sent by one of the captives
(Fantees) a symbolical message to the Governor,
consisting of two sticks, one short and the other
long, and requested him to make his choice.　If he
took the short one, he was to give up the Ashantee
runaways, and the war would be at once at an end ;
but if he retained the long one, he, the Prince, would
continue the war for the next three years amidst all
difficulties.　Mr. Pine retained the *long stick*, and
sent to inform the Ashantee general that he was
prepared to prosecute the war for the next seven
years, until the kingdom of Ashantee should be
prostrated before the English Government.

The Ashantee general-in-chief, knowing from experience how disastrous it is to keep a large army in
the field during the rainy season, principally from
climatic affections, quietly withdrew into his own
territory.; and, after disbanding most of his men, he
quartered a few in the principal high roads to the
kingdom.

Governor Pine, shocked at the unsatisfactory
termination of the war, from which a great deal of
good to the Protectorate had been expected, was
seriously taken ill in the camp, and was brought
down almost lifeless to Cape Coast.　The regular

troops returned to winter (rainy season) quarters within the forts on the sea-coast towns, and the native force returned each man to his own home.

Thus terminated the first Ashantee campaign.

I have the honour to be,

Your Lordship's most obedient Servant,

J. A. B. HORTON, M.D.

LETTER No. V.*

TO THE RIGHT HON. EARL GRANVILLE, K.G., D.C.L.,
SECRETARY OF STATE FOR THE COLONIES,
&c., &c., &c.

CAPE COAST CASTLE,
12th December, 1869.

MY LORD,

Whilst the campaign was being vigorously
prosecuted by both parties with different modes of
manœuvring, an episode (which tended in a great
measure to explain the feelings of the Fantees under
English rule towards those under the Dutch rule)
occurred which is worth recording. In April, 1863,
when the whole of the Ashantee forces were in
British territory, His Excellency Colonel Elias, the
Dutch Governor, was in active correspondence with
the Commander-in-Chief of the Ashantee army.
One of his letters was intercepted. It was addressed
—" To the Captain-General of the Ashantee army
at war against the British ;" and although it was not
opened on the coast, yet still the very fact of the
correspondence having taken place caused a good

---

* Reply dated 18th January, 1870.

deal of ill-will amongst the Fantees against the Dutch. On the 17th of August, the same year, King Quacoe Duah sent through the English Governor some 150 Dutch subjects, natives of Elmina, who had been residing in Coomassie for mercantile purposes, requesting him to forward them to Elmina, as they belonged to a neutral Government. The Dutch Government, during the great wars between Ashantee and the British authorities, extending over ten years, including the years between 1820 and 1830, when the two great and disastrous battles of Essamacow and Doodoowah were fought—disastrous, the one to the Ashantees, the other to the British, when Sir Charles McCarthy and others were killed—not only received the Ashantees with open arms, but also sold powder and other munitions of war secretly to them. All these acts have produced in the British Fantees an irreconcilable barrier against any friendship or unity between them and the Dutch Fantees so long as they remain under Dutch rule and allied to the Ashantees.

The utter failure of the campaign, described in my last letter, led to cries and meetings of indignation against the commander of the expeditionary force, and petitions to the Governor were presented, praying him to put a pressure on the home authorities, that prompt, adequate, and efficient measures might then be adopted to clear the Gold Coast territory from all future troubles with their powerful neighbours, the Ashantees.

In consequence of strong representations from the Coast, the Government of Lord Palmerston ordered from the West Indies the 4th West India Regiment to the Gold Coast. About 450 rank and file, under Lieutenant-Colonel Couran, in H.M. troop-ship "Magæra," landed at Cape Coast Castle on the 13th August, 1863. The Gold Coast Artillery Corps were disbanded, and active preparations set on foot for taking the field. In December the first movement of the regulars for the field took place. The officer commanding divided his army into three divisions, to each of which were to be attached hereafter 7,000 local militia volunteers and native allies. A depôt for the supply of the whole camp was formed at Mansoo, a place situated equi-distant between the sea-coast and the frontiers of the kingdom of Ashantee.

The first division of the regular army, under Captain Mackay, left Cape Coast about the 27th or

28th of December, and arrived at Mansoo on the
1st January, 1864, where they were employed in
building fortifications and clearing the bush around.
A few weeks afterwards the detachment of soldiers
at Accra received orders to move to Akim Swadrue,
and join a detachment of men who had been sent
there to protect the road.   On the 25th January, at
three p.m., the second battalion of the first division
of the army (4th West India Regiment) and the
first battalion of the third division, composed of the
2nd West India Regiment, under Captain Knapp,
left Cape Coast amidst the cheers of the population.
They arrived at Mansoo on the 31st.   On the
morning of the 30th, Governor Pine, having previously delivered over the entire military control of
the Protectorate into the hands of Lieutenant-
Colonel Couran, commanding the troops, that officer,
with his staff and the remainder of the force at Cape
Coast, composed of a part of the 4th and 2nd West
India Regiments, left the Castle for the Praah. The
soldiers were in high spirits, determined

> " With rifle, gun, and sword in hand,
>   To carry through Ashantee's crowd,
>   Our colours to Coomassie."

They arrived at Mansoo on the 1st, and left on the

3rd, arriving at the Praah on the 5th February. The army had to pass through dense and thickly-wooded forests; at times they had to plunge into ravines of great depth, where the pestiferous exhalations of a humid soil steamed up amidst the incense of sweet-scented flowers, which shone through the deep gloom in every conceivable variety of colour. Here in some parts were extensive pools of water, which they had to wade knee and sometimes neck deep, to the great prejudice of discipline and good order; there a rapid and deep stream without a bridge over it, to be crossed in the best way each one could. Whilst passing through the forest, birds rivalling the fantastic variety of flowers, presented tints as brilliant and as beautiful as any of the vegetable world; above their heads were chattering monkeys making grimaces, which occasioned not a little merriment amongst them; here and there were hideous reptiles of every shape, hue, and kind, from the gigantic boa, performing amusing gyrations amongst the lofty trees around, down to the alligators, which basked leisurely in the sun.

Fifteen days before the first movement of the regular force took place, a company composed of

fifty men from the late Gold Coast Artillery Corps
was organized by the Colonial Government, and
placed under the command of Captain Hay, and
ordered to march to Appolonia, the most western
frontier of the Protectorate, and there serve as a
corps of observation.

At the commencement of the military movements, His Excellency Governor Pine received
orders from the home authorities not to act on the
offensive against the Ashantees, but to remain on the
defensive. Subsequently his orders were that, if he
found that he could not make a lasting peace without an offensive movement on the enemies' territory,
he was to march to Coomassie. They therefore
placed at his disposal about 600 additional forces,
making a total of 1,290 men ;—viz, 900 of the 4th
West India Regiment, 170 of the 2nd, and 220 of
the 1st.

The troops, after arriving at the Praah, commenced the building of an extensive stockade, and
cleared the forest around the camp, as well as that
in the enemies' country before the camp. The
"Tamar" troop-ship, with the contingent of men
expected, arrived on the 9th April, and 200 were
detached and dispatched to the frontier. About this

time the season had advanced, the rains had set in, and the river Praah had swollen considerably. Since the arrival of the troops on the enemies' frontier in January last, six months before, not an enemy had been seen; both officers and men who had served or were serving in the bush in camp, without any active engagement, were laid prostrate by climatic diseases, principally dysentery and fever; the mortality amongst the officers and men who served in the bush was enormous, so that most of the troops were recalled from the interior. The debate in Parliament relative to the Ashantee war led to the entire withdrawal of the troops from the interior, and the embarkation of most of the men for the West Indies.

Thus terminated the second campaign against the King of Ashantee, which was by no means better than the first, as it left the original question in a worse state than it ever was, and the King of Ashantee in a position of moral conquest.

Confusion now reigned in the whole of the Protectorate; the prestige of the ruling power suffered fearfully; the inhabitants of the Gold Coast were, for the first time, distinctly told that, in case of an invasion, they were to be left to protect themselves,

unless when the coast or towns in the immediate vicinity of our forts were attacked ; trade was
stopped, and several of the merchants became bank-
rupts, and others in a state next to it.

Since the termination of the campaign in June,
1864, abortive attempts have frequently been made
to establish a reconciliation between the Ashantees
and the British Government.   The most important
negotiation on the subject was made about the
latter end of 1866, when, through the influence of
the Honourable George Blankson, a native merchant of Anamaboe, during the government of
Colonel Couran, ambassadors with sixty-five re-
tainers were sent to his Excellency the Lieutenant-
Governor to consider terms of peace.   On the 16th
January, a proclamation was issued, setting forth
that, from communications received from Coomassie,
through four duly accredited ambassadors of the
King of Ashantee, dated 19th and 20th December,
1865, and the 8th January, 1866, soliciting peace
between his kingdom and the British Protectorate,
peace was therefore declared and proclaimed.   The
King of Ashantee was indignant when he heard
that the proclamation set forth that he had sued for
peace.   He emphatically declared that it was the

Governor, through his agent, who had commenced the peace negotiation, and that he now declined to continue the correspondence unless Gamin be first given up. Through these circumstances the attempt at settling the Ashantee difficulties met with an untimely end, and the confusion between Ashantee and Fantee remained *in statu quo*.

Hitherto I have said nothing whatever about the eastern district of the Gold Coast, which comprises nationalities that took no active part in the disturbances of the western district,—viz., the Accras, Aquapims, Crobboes, Creepees, and Adangmes. They remained around their own hearths enjoying their peaceful avocations. A few days after this delusive proclamation was posted up for public good, war was declared between the Accras and the Awoonahs, who resided on the other side of the river Volta, beyond the present boundary of the Protectorate.

The Awoonahs, under the command of one Geraldo, a notorious slave-dealer, for some trifling misunderstanding which happened eight months before, attacked Adah, a town within the Protectorate, situated at the mouth of the river Volta; seized the canoes, burnt Kporng, the great emporium for cotton, and midway town between Accra and Creepee, and destroyed a large quantity of goods. Geraldo, having selected a very favourable point as the base of his operations, put an entire stop to the trade through the Volta river. Tidings of the daring pertinacity of the slave-dealer caused anger and cries for revenge throughout the whole of the mercantile community of Accra, and representations were made to the Lieutenant-Governor to interfere and to compel the Awoonahs to give up Geraldo, and thus put an end to any further trouble in the matter.

After some futile attempts at negotiation had taken place, war was declared by the Accras against the Awoonahs, and a large force, to the number of some 20,000 men, was gathered at the plains of Adah. Colonel Couran, Lieutenant-Governor, supplied the expeditionary force with 1,200 muskets and about fifty kegs of ball cartridge, the whole native force being under the command of Lieut. Herbert, civil commandant of the eastern district. The expeditionary force started from Accra on the 18th February, 1866 ; on the 18th March they were joined in the plains of Malamfie (which was selected as the base of operations) by 50 regulars of the 3rd

West India Regiment. under Captain Hamilton, who, being the senior officer in camp, took over the command of the whole expedition. He gave orders to the chiefs to carry out certain judicious measures as preliminary to the final march on the enemy's territory, but they refused point blank to obey his orders. He immediately withdrew from the camp with his men, having no power to punish them, and he left Lieut. Herbert in command.

After making some preliminary arrangements, on the 25th March a force of about 15,000 men crossed to the left or Awoonah bank of the river Volta. On the 3rd April they marched from Ado-domey and reached Tojay, a branch of the Volta, which they crossed on the 4th, and encamped at an extensive grove of palm trees. Here they remained until the 12th, and in a council of war it was decided that they should advance direct on the capital, Awoonah, on the sea-coast, which was about six hours' march. After marching about two hours, whilst passing through a narrow defile, surrounded by thick bush, the Awoonahs, about 8,000 strong, who had lain in ambush, suddenly opened fire on the leading men, and threw them into confusion. The Awoonahs now advanced and fired rapidly;

the guns, rockets, luggage, and everything were abandoned by the allied force, and there was a disastrous panic in the whole camp. The allied force, 15,000 strong, were mercilessly shot down, caught alive, and driven in utter confusion by 8,000 of the Awoonahs in the field. The day was inevitably lost ; the guns and rockets were captured and recaptured by both parties ; and, but for the timely arrival of Quow Daddy, King of Aquapim, with his army of 4,000 strong, which opened fire on the Awoonahs in their rear, a most fearful slaughter of the whole of the allied force would have taken place. The panic-stricken army, the next morning becoming disorganized and dispirited, disobeyed the orders of the commander to advance against the enemy or halt ; but they made a precipitous retreat to the Volta, where they arrived on the 13th (Friday) April, 1866, and crossed the next day. Every man now found his way home as best he could ; and thus ended the campaign against the Awoonahs.*

---

* A most faithful and extensive account of this Awoonah campaign is to be found in a letter addressed to the *African Times*, published in its number of September 22nd, 1866, page 28, which we quote as follows :—

In February the Governor (Colonel Couran) determined to

In October, the Governor, accompanied by two of the merchants of Accra, went to Jellee Coffee, the head-quarters of the Awoonahs, for the express purpose of endeavouring to come to some amicable settlement of the whole affair. They proposed to the Awoonahs that Geraldo should be given up, and that 2,000 dollars should be paid by them on account of the expenses incurred by the Accras through the war. To this the Awoonahs, who were victorious in the last expedition, rejoined that they could not deliver up Geraldo, he being a stranger in the country; and that they, being the greatest sufferers in the war, could not afford to pay any indemnity. There was nothing decisive agreed upon, and the matter rested in this unsatisfactory state.

The Ashantees, hearing of what had taken place in the eastern district between the inhabitants of the Protectorate and their neighbours, must needs dip their fingers into the pie. The King of Ashantee sent messengers to the Aquamboos and

---

assist in the expedition against Geraldo and his band of robbers. After having issued out 1,200 old muskets and some fifty kegs of damaged ball cartridge to Kings Cudjoe, of Jamestown, and Dawoonah, of Christiansborg, he gave them three days to start and take the field, under pain of taking away the arms, &c., should

Awoonahs, offering them his assistance. The messengers took the great oath as to the truth of their mission; the Awoonahs sent hostages to the king

---

they not leave within that time. This hurrying the people on so fast was the first error, and a very great one in the late affair. The consequence was that, on the morning of Sunday, February 18, when Lieutenant Herbert, the civil commandant, commander-in-chief of the expedition, started from Jamestown with King Cudjoe, there was not a soul that accompanied them but Mr. John Smith, of Jamestown, who had charge of the rockets and guns, and Mr. E. Bannerman, who had volunteered as adjutant-general and private secretary to the commander-in-chief, and the four men who carried Cudjoe's basket of state. At 5 p.m. on that day this party reached Pram Pram, twenty-eight miles from Accra. On the 19th, at 6 p.m., these were joined at Pram Pram by Mr. Irvine and Mr. Clayton (the only English merchants who had engaged personally in the war, besides furnishing large supplies of money and materials), and two other of the Bannermans, with about 200 men, whom these four had equipped as volunteers, and tolerably well disciplined. The time fixed for stopping at Pram Pram was two days, and thought to be sufficient for enabling the whole of King Cudjoe's men to join; but it was nine days before the expedition could proceed, and then with only 400 men, to Ningo, the next town on the route to Addah, only eight miles from Pram Pram. There it waited three days for the Jamestown people. But King Dawoonah's force had taken the inland route; and the expedition, which up to that time had marched along the seashore, intending to go by the beach to Addah, at the mouth of the Volta, joined him on the 1st of March at Kanar, which was the place of general rendezvous. There the whole force remained for seventeen days, doing nothing. Kanar is about four hours' foot journey from Addah, and two hours from Melamfie on the Volta, opposite to which town, on the Awoonah side, Geraldo had encamped. The

and accepted his offer. He immediately dispatched a large army to their assistance, which commenced operations against the Creepees and Agotins, two

---

whole force at Kanar on 1st March only mustered 800 men; by the 8th, the Jamestown and Christiansborg people had joined their chief, besides the natives of Pram Pram, another of King Cudjoe's towns, which gave 3,000 armed men. On the 11th and 12th, the natives of the Accra towns, under Dawoonah—viz., Labaddy, Teshie, Tenmah, and Poney—mustering 3,000 more, joined. During this period they had been in communication with the doubtful tribes in the vicinity, most of whom had already eaten fetish with Geraldo to fight for him, but seeing the large force preparing against him had begun to waver. Lieutenant Herbert, thinking his force sufficient to take the field, dispatched Mr. Irvine and Mr. Clayton to Addah to muster 100 large canoes and convey them from Addah to Melamfie, to transport the force across the Volta to attack the enemy. Through the usual dilatoriness of the natives, it was four days before they could report that they were ready to start from Addah, with only sixty-five canoes. Accordingly, on Saturday, the 17th March, at 6 P.M., Lieut. Herbert, with his 6,000 men, marched to Melamfie, which was found to be quite deserted, the inhabitants having gone across to the enemy, who were encamped exactly opposite the place (the river is there about 400 yards wide); but one man was captured, who with another had been left to watch; the other escaped by swimming across the river, although at least fifty shots were fired at him. The enemy returned the fire, which was quite harmless, Geraldo himself firing his Minié rifle. This man was recognized at once, standing in a very prominent position. In consequence of the very difficult nature of the ground from Kanor to Melamfie, it was 3 P.M. before the rockets and field-pieces came up, under the charge of Mr. Smith. On his arrival, Lieutenant Herbert directed him to throw a shell and rockets into Geraldo's camp. The first rocket destroyed half their

tribes in the interior, allied to the Accras. Whilst this negotiation was going on, about the 27th April, 1867, died suddenly in his capital, King Quacoe

---

camp, a very extensive one. The enemy must have suffered great damage this first day without loss to us. On the 18th, at 11 A.M., Mr. Irvine arrived with 800 Addahs in sixty-five canoes, escorted by a guard of fifty men of the 3rd West India Regiment, under Captain Humphrey and Lieutenant Stewart, with Dr. Davies, S.A.S. (a native), in medical charge, a rocket, and one howitzer. On Captain Humphrey's arrival he, as senior to Lieutenant Herbert, assumed the chief command, and directed Mr. Smith and Lieutenant Stewart, with their guns and rockets, to shell and destroy the remaining portion of the enemy's camp. This was very speedily effected. Captain Humphrey, observing that Geraldo had several large English canoes and boats hauled up on the opposite bank, called for fifty volunteers to proceed across the river and take possession of them. These fifty men, furnished by Messrs. Hesse, Briand, Addi, and Bannerman, joined by 150 Addahs, crossed over in sixteen canoes, and, though opposed by some 300 of Geraldo's men posted on an eminence, made good their landing, drove the enemy from their position, killing large numbers; but, instead of carrying out their orders, and bringing away the canoes and boats, they pursued the flying enemy inland, until the latter were largely reinforced, and drove them back.

They succeeded, however, in bringing off with them six large canoes, but at the very moment of pushing off another canoe, which contained the head chief of Addah, was upset, and the enemy, being secreted in thick bushes within ten yards, picked off this chief and four of his principal captains, and some dozen inferior men; these were killed outright, and some thirty-six more were wounded. (Through the skill of Dr. Davies every wounded man has since recovered.) This affair had a bad effect on the whole campaign, as from that day the Addahs had no leaders. On the 20th the remainder of the

Duah, the most peaceful and wise ruler of the kingdom of Ashantee, and was buried in the mausoleum of the kings amidst the most revolting

---

force reached the camp. Quow Daddy, King of Aquapim, a very brave man, but most bloodthirsty and cruel, arrived with 4,000 men. His men were by far the best in the field, being most amenable and obedient to authority and their king. King Tackee, the king of the whole eastern districts, but residing in Dutch (!) Accra, also arrived on the same day with about 4,000 men—bringing up the force to over 16,000. With this large force, Captain Humphrey decided to cross at once, and sent a body of Addahs over at daylight, on the 21st, to establish themselves on a hill to the left of the enemy's position, so as to withdraw their attention, whilst the main body crossed in their front. The Addahs gained their position without being opposed, and immediately sent one canoe back with the information that the enemy had entirely vanished. Order was then at an end. Capt. Humphrey then wished to start in pursuit of the enemy at once, with the view of effecting the capture of Geraldo, who, it was reported, had been severely wounded by the bursting of a shell. But the people, who looked more upon King Tackee as the commander-in-chief than upon Captain Humphrey, grumbled and growled and hesitated. Captain Humphrey then gave orders for 2,000 men to occupy the position recently vacated by the enemy ; this order the chiefs all, with the exception of Dawoonah, of Christiansborg, refused to obey. Dawoonah, who is a very sensible old man, educated in Copenhagen some forty years ago by the Danish Government, ordered his men across the river, intending to go himself, with his tent, &c., next day, saying that he, as a British subject, would not recognize the authority of a king living under the Dutch flag, and who had brought Dutch flags to the campaign. This created much ill-feeling in the camp ; and, as nearly the whole of the other towns sided with Tackee, the Dutchman, they compelled Dawoonah to recall his men

massacre of the population. He reigned twenty-
seven years, and was succeeded by his nephew,
Coffee Culcary, a fiery young man of thirty-five, and

---

from the other side. *Captain Humphrey, seeing this done in open
defiance of his authority, at once left for Addah with his detachment,
leaving the expedition in charge of Lieut. Herbert.* Lieut. Herbert
called a general meeting of all the chiefs, and told them plainly that
if they refused to obey his orders, and chose to look to the King of
Dutch Accra as their chief, he also would leave them, and take
away the guns and rockets, and that the Europeans and native
gentlemen would accompany him. They then promised willing
obedience from that day. But as he had not one regular soldier
with him, he had no power to enforce obedience.

On the 22nd, Mr. Irvine left Melamfie for Accra and Cape Coast,
deputed to apply to the Governor for a further supply of ammunition, and, in case of refusal, to purchase some. Mr. Clayton, being
sick, left with him, both on horseback.

Melamfie is eighty miles from Accra, through a most magnificent
country, but nothing to eat on the road till you reach Pram Pram.

On the 23rd, 24th, and 25th, the whole force crossed over and
encamped at a place called Adodomay, exactly opposite Melamfie.
During the period from the 20th to the 25th, some twenty stragglers,
belonging to Melamfie, who had joined Geraldo, but had deserted
him, were caught. All these the chiefs nominally under Lieut.
Herbert executed in cold blood, as soon as they found that they
had fought on the opposite side on the previous Sunday. Their
heads were cut off, and the skulls having been cleaned, were fixed
to the drums as trophies!!! Three men that were caught on the
day of the enemy's retreat were rescued by Mr. Edmund Bannerman, as Lieut. Herbert had issued orders that no one should be
killed without being first brought to him. As he was conducting
them to that part of the camp where he was quartered, some of the
crowd following (about 5,000 men) recognized them as three of the

the old feud between Coomassie and the protected
territory was vigorously kept up.

Since the peace negotiations of Colonel Couran

---

principal of Geraldo's supporters, two of them being blacksmiths
who had been engaged for six months casting Minié bullets for him;
the third, a fetish-man who used to make fetish for him!—for he
believed in it. In less than fifteen seconds their heads were off,
all Mr. Bannerman's efforts to save them being unavailing; and he
had himself a narrow escape, as the people, in their eagerness to kill
them, were not particular as to the direction in which they struck.

The scenes in camp at this time were truly awful. The cutting
off of heads and the mutilation of bodies, and leaving them to be
disposed of by turkey buzzards and patakoos (hyenas), dreadful as
all this was, were by no means the most painful sights.

One day our people heard that the wives and children of the
Melamfies, those who had sided with Geraldo and fought against
them, were hiding in the bush close to Melamfie, near their camp.

Some 800 of them at once proceeded to the spot, and captured
the whole, consisting of about 500 women and children, of from
twelve years down to infants. These, however, turned out to be
not Melamfies, but belonging to neutral tribes, who, in fear, had
hidden their families in this way. The Commandant, on this being
reported to him by King Dawoonah, directed Mr. Hesse and Mr.
E. Bannerman to go to every chief and demand the restoration of
all these poor creatures thus taken by their people. In this manner
about 450 were recovered. The scene that took place when these
450 were all collected in front of the Commandant's quarters was
truly painful. Mothers who had been separated from their suckling
infants, and children who had lost their parents, thus meeting again,
and still uncertain of their ultimate fate (for the men taken with
them had been decapitated in their presence), and embracing and
clinging to each other, the whole weeping and wailing in a manner
that might dissolve stones, but could not, and did not, have the

and the two Accra merchants, it was arranged that everything was to be left until the arrival of the Governor-General.   On the 6th April, 1867, he

---

slightest effect on the persons who had originally panyarred them, and were eagerly watching for any want of vigilance to retake them. It was in truth a most painful sight.   There were many of these women and children carried off by the Addahs and Accras before we could interfere.   I should think that upwards of 100 so disappeared; and some who ought to have been above such dealings participated in the horrid plunder.   Those that were released were restored to their homes.   With regard to the execution of prisoners in cold blood, the act itself perhaps was not so much to be blamed as the horrible and cruel mode in which it was carried out.   Most of those that were decapitated were deserving of death properly inflicted.   For instance, all the Melamfies who were caught with arms in hands should have been hung at once, and would in most instances have been so hung had they been brought before the proper authorities; but they were generally decapitated as soon as they were recognized as Melamfies.   They may have deserved death for this reason: Melamfie is in the Protectorate, on this side the Volta. The Melamfies are naturally allies of the Addahs, and therefore of Accra also.   They took ammunition from the Addahs for the purpose of aiding them to fight against Geraldo.   They also received some from Geraldo with which they actually fought against the Addahs, &c.   Had they joined the Addahs, or even remained neutral, Geraldo could have given no trouble to the country. When the allied forces arrived in Kanar Camp they came and offered to join.   The night before the force left Kanar for Melamfie, they decamped and gave Geraldo full information of all movements. Had the people captured a *bonâ fide* Awoonah man they would never have executed him.   They would either keep him as a slave, or let his family ransom him.   In the heat of battle they sometimes do kill prisoners, but not always.

By the evening of the 25th, some 16,000 men were all on the

(Major Blackhall) anchored off Accra roadstead ; heard the complaints of the merchants and people ; proceeded down to Jellee Coffee with the Adminis-

---

Awoonah bank of the river Volta. By the 1st April the force was weeded of some thousand or so cowards who did not relish going into the heart of the enemy's country, and disappeared. On the 3rd April the force marched from Adodomay to attack the enemy, supposed to have encamped about a day's march from that place. On the 4th it reached the river Tojay, a branch of the Volta, and, having crossed it, encamped in an immense grove of palm trees. The camp here was for once formed in regular order, especially that of the Aquapims.

It took four hours to visit the whole camp, hurriedly even. The force halted there till the 12th, when it advanced with the intention of going direct to the sea-coast town of Awoonah, the capital of Awoonah, and residence of the king and head fetish. It was supposed to be 'six hours' journey. After marching about two hours very slovenly, with rocket-tube and field-piece in front, the Awoonahs, 8,000 strong, suddenly pounced upon the expedition in a place most favourable to them—a very narrow defile surrounded by thick bush. The enemy had possession of the bush in front and on each flank. Their first fire threw the leading men (most of whom were carriers of luggage) into great confusion ; these falling back got mixed up with the women carrying loads. It was a regular surprise. The Commandant, with most of the native gentlemen, were actually sitting down in front close to the gun when the first musket was fired by the enemy. Unfortunately, the carriers of the ammunition for the rocket-tube and howitzer were nowhere to be found. The enemy advancing rapidly, there was no help for it but to abandon gun, rocket, baggage, and everything. A complete panic ensued; not a shot could be fired without hitting our own people. Our men were being shot down, cut down, and caught alive without resistance. Here we were, 15,000 men, who boasted of having conquered the Ashantees, well-armed and no doubt brave, flying before at most

trator ; received on board his yacht John Tay, merchant of that place, and a chief of a small hamlet called Sroghey.   The whole Palaver was entered into, and Major Blackhall, the Governor-General pointed out to them the evils of war and the good they would derive by having peace. These people made protestations whilst on board of sincere contrition, and agreed to and signed a treaty of peace on behalf of the Awoonahs.   This treaty was only worth the paper on which it was written, inasmuch as

---

8,000 Awoonahs, whose only bullets were small stones ! It was disgraceful.   All efforts to check the flight were in vain.   A few, especially the Dutch Accras, made a stand, and suffered most severely in consequence, but it checked the enemy.   At length, Quow Daddy, the King of Aquapim, who had with his 4,000 brave men taken a different line of march, got to the rear of the Awoonahs, and placed them in their own trap.   They then began to turn, and finally threw away their arms and fled, being pursued by the Aquapims and a few Accras.   These slaughtered them like sheep.   Notwithstanding all this turn of the tide at least 5,000 of our men continued their flight.   The whole affair lasted only three or four hours.   During this period the gun was captured and recaptured a dozen times.   When the Awoonahs first seized it, one of them jumped up on the top of it and began to dance.   He was at once shot down.   Another took his place.   He was shot ; and so on until ten had been so killed.   Then they fought hand to hand for the gun until they were finally driven away.   We lost about 65 killed and 320 wounded, and, as we had now no Dr. Davis, at least 150 of these subsequently died.   The enemy was pursued almost as far as Jellee Coffee and Awoonah.   Nothing had now to be done but to follow

at the very time of signature and subsequently, the
Awoonahs, with their allies the Aquamboos and
Ashantees, were committing the grossest acts of
robbery, murder, and pillage in the Protectorate,
had entirely stopped the navigation of the Volta
and blockaded the roads to Creepee, and had formed
an alliance offensive and defensive with the Ashantees, who were in arms against the Protectorate.

From the statements contained in this and the
last letter, it is evident that the political atmosphere

---

them up with the whole force, and finish the war at one blow. But
the morning's panic had totally disorganized and dispirited the whole
force. They declined to obey the orders of Lieutenant Herbert,
either to advance or halt. They preferred retreat. The chiefs also
were not unanimous. King Quow Daddy was so annoyed at this
conduct on the part of his allies, that he at once struck his camp and
marched his brave army direct home, leading himself on foot, a fine,
tall, handsome man. The rest of the army, having confidence in no
one else but Quow Daddy and his people, at once followed. This
was on the morning of Friday, the 13th. The same evening we
reached the Volta, and crossed it next day. We then proceeded to
Addah with our rockets and guns; the majority of the army had left
their chiefs and gone home. The chiefs went with us to Addah.
Lieutenant Herbert finding this was the state of affairs, and being
sick, left for Accra, placing the command of such an army as was left
in the hands of Mr. Hesse, who, with the other gentlemen that were left
with him, arrived five days after in Accra, leaving the three kings of
Accra (Jamestown, Dutch, and Christiansborg), who with their
principal captains were still at Addah, where they were determined,
they said, to remain till Geraldo was captured. Thus ended the first
campaign against Geraldo and the Awoonahs!

of the Gold Coast territory, when the ratification of treaty between the Courts of St. James's and the Hague took place on the 1st January, 1868, was in a very unsatisfactory condition. The feelings of the whole Fantee race were in a state of morbid irritation ; and although peace with Ashantee was looked for with great anxiety, yet still they refrained from accepting a humiliating peace. The complications with the neighbouring tribes about Accra, which terminated in hostilities inglorious to the inhabitants of the eastern district, were still pending. The Dutch having kept up friendly intercourse with Ashantee during the whole of their misunderstanding with Fantee, and having acted as the latter considered in a manner hostile to their interest, were in great disfavour with the whole of the tribes under British rule. The country was in this state when, during the transfer of territory, the outrage on Commendah was committed, and the whole of the British Fantees in the western district, unlike their usual procrastination, rose as one man against the Dutch.

I have the honour to be, Sir,

Your most obedient Servant,

J. A. B. HORTON, M.D.

LETTER No. VI.*

TO THE RIGHT HON. EARL GRANVILLE, K.G., D.C.L.,
SECRETARY OF STATE FOR THE COLONIES,
&c., &c., &c.

THE CASTLE, CAPE COAST,
12*th January*, 1870.

MY LORD,

After the retreat of the large force encamped around Elmina, as detailed in my letter
No. III., each division of the army, according to their
province, retired to their own homes, and the Elmina
difficulties remained for a time *in statu quo*, until
His Excellency Sir Arthur Kennedy, the Governor-
General, paid his first visit to this part of the coast.
During this time, however, many small marauding
expeditions were taken for the express purpose of
plunder by each contending army. One or more
small, unprotected villages generally fell within their
reach, and cold-blooded murder, with the plunder
of a few trifling articles, was the result of their
midnight raid. Engagements at sea were not un-

---

* Reply through Administrator of the Gold Coast in Dispatch
No. 116, dated 28th February, 1870.

frequent. Sometimes canoes from one Dutch settlement were waylaid and attacked, their contents pillaged, and the men taken as prisoners; another time, a number of fishing canoes of the Fantees would suddenly make to and attack the same or less number of Dutch fish canoes. The result of these mimic engagements were invariably in favour of the former parties.

His Excellency Sir Arthur Kennedy, Governor-in-Chief, arrived at Cape Coast on the 27th October, 1868, in H.M.S. "Lee," and immediately took measures to make himself thoroughly acquainted with the subject of dispute between the English and Dutch Fantees, and then proceeded to adopt the most feasible method of putting a stop the misunderstanding. He repaired to Elmina, and with Governor Boers* convened a meeting of both Dutch and native authorities. He informed them that, being well acquainted from documentary and other evidences of all the *pros* and *cons* of the quarrel between the Dutch and English Fantees, he had personally appeared before them not to discuss the point in dispute, but to arrange matters amicably

---

* Dutch Governor of Elmina.

between them, and therefore proposed, in a most statesmanlike manner, that in consequence of the exchange of territory between the two civilized Governments on the Coast, which had led to a great change in the political position of the neighbouring independent tribe, viz., Ashantee, it behoved the people on the sea-coast to be united in one common bond for mutual support, offensive and defensive. A treaty based on these conditions was the only means by which a lasting peace could be secured to the countries under British and Dutch Protectorate. The tall, fine, majestic figure of Sir Arthur Kennedy, with his silvery locks, urbanity of manners, decisive and rather imperious tone, struck the natives with a sort of veneration or reverential awe, and brought vividly into their recollection the like stateliness of Sir Charles McCarthy, who was killed at the battle of Essamacow. The Elmina chiefs retired from the council chamber to consult and frame a fitting reply to His Excellency's proposal. The Dutch Governor, perhaps observing the effect of the earnest appeal of the Governor-General on the Elmina king and chiefs, sent one of his officers to join them in their consultation, and so to dictate to them what reply suitable to the wishes of the

Dutch Governor they should return. The chiefs refused *in toto* to ally themselves offensively and defensively with the English Fantees and give up paying tribute to Ashantee, and they further stated plainly that they preferred the friendship of the latter nation.

Sir Arthur Kennedy now denounced their conduct and that of the Dutch authorities as being open to the gravest reprehension, and then retired from the council hall, and embarked soon afterwards for Cape Coast. He informed the chiefs of Fantee of the result of his interference, and told them that they were at liberty to undertake any expedition against the Dutch Fantees.*

---

* In November, 1868, a Memorial, setting forth the state and feelings of the country, drawn up by Wm. Cleaver, Esq., agent of Messrs. F. and A. Swanzy, was intended to have been presented to Sir Arthur Kennedy, C.B., Governor-in-Chief of the West African Settlements, but which, unfortunately, was not forwarded; but as it treated on points of great interest with respect to the transfer of territory, I shall here quote it *verbatim et literatim :—*

" The Memorial of the kings, chiefs, &c., of Her Majesty's possessions on the Gold Coast—Respectfully showeth :—

" That the convention between Her Majesty and the King of the Netherlands for an interchange of territory on the Gold Coast of Africa, signed at London, March 5, 1867, has produced most disastrous results to your Memorialists, involving sacrifice of human life and the peace of the country at present and formerly connected with your Excellency's Government.

Since the defeat of the Accras in the Trans-
voltine expedition and the peace proclamation of
Governor Blackhall, the eastern district had remained in a state of the most turbulent confusion :
small fights had occasionally taken place, men, women,
and children were caught and beheaded, trade was
stopped, and in fact every thing had been in utter
confusion and dismay. The arrival of Sir Arthur
Kennedy on the 10th November was hailed with
joy. He had several interviews with the chiefs and
merchants relative to the disturbances at the Volta.
Whilst at Accra he was met by Captain Glover,
who arrived in his steamer the " Eyo." This indefatigable Governor of Lagos, whose indomitable

---

" That your Memorialists protested against the cession by Her
Majesty of all British forts, possessions, and rights of sovereignty or
jurisdiction which she possessed on the Gold Coast to the westward
of the mouth of the Sweet River, for that the people of the aforesaid
territory have, from time immemorial, been allies of your Memorialists against all enemies, and fought with them against the
Ashantees by the aid of Her Majesty's troops with success.

" That the people to the westward of the Sweet River aforesaid,
enjoying the protection and patronage of Her Majesty, also protested against the convention.

" That your Memorialists and their allies were in hostilities with
the Ashantees at the date of the convention, and that no settlement
of their difficulties has yet been arranged.

" That the protests of your Memorialists and others concerned
were ignored, and that the Dutch Government commenced coercive

perseverance and real hard work has raised that
infant colony to the state of progressive civilization
which confers great credit on him, left soon after-

---

measures against the people formerly under Her Majesty's protection ; consequently your Memorialists, in accordance with the terms
of their alliance, immediately proceeded to the assistance of their
allies, and, for injuries received, determined to compel the people of
the Dutch to join the alliance of all the powers south of the River
Prah against further invasions or encroachments of the Ashantees.
Hence the difficulties which, up to the present time, have baffled all
the exertions of the officers administering Her Majesty's Government.

"That the Dutch Government has for many years past paid
tribute annually to the King of the Ashantees, and been strongly
allied to that power, which in peaceful times supplied slaves to the
Dutch Government, who shipped them to Java.

"That during the Ashantee invasions against your Memorialists
and their allies, the people under the Dutch Government have proposed neutrality. But during the war of 1824 they betrayed the
trust of your Memorialists and some of their people to Elmina for
safety. The property, consisting of gold dust, gold ornaments, &c.,
was never returned ; some of the people were killed, and others sold
as slaves. From that time your Memorialists and their allies have
always mistrusted the people under Dutch rule, and had good
reason to believe that they assisted the Ashantees with munitions of
war during hostilities, and further suspected them of intrigues with
that power.

"That the Dutch possessions on the Gold Coast, up to the date
of the convention, were insignificant compared to those of Her
Majesty. The Dutch possessed no inland territory, while Her
Majesty's possessions extended north, east, and west of the Dutch,
confining them to the seaboard.

"That your Memorialists, having represented the insignificance of

wards for the Volta, and succeeded in crossing the bar of the river with his steamer, which is the first that has ever entered it. This movement, important

the Dutch possessions, beg your Excellency to consider the unpleasant relations of the people of those places with your Memorialists in time of invasion of their country by the Ashantees. At such a time it would be most embarrassing to have to contend with an enemy in the rear.

"That your Excellency is acquainted with the importance of the alliance of all the people under both Governments against the Ashantees. And your Memorialists hoped your endeavours to arrange it on the occasion of your last visit to the seat of this Government and that of the Dutch (viz., Elmina) would be successful; but, unfortunately, your Memorialists were disappointed.

"They fully expected your Excellency would be successful, for they had reason to believe the Elminas and others were at last willing to join the alliance, and believe they would have done so but for the opposition of the Dutch Government.

"That the opposition of the Dutch Government to an alliance of their people with your Memorialists and others emanates from their connexion with the Ashantee power, who supply slaves for export as aforesaid.

"That the people who now refuse to become our allies are connected with us by family ties; and, from the close proximity of the territories of both Governments, we are at a loss to understand why they continue obstinate unless by the direction of their Government.

"That your Memorialists being satisfied that the proposed general alliance will secure permanent peace by destroying the hopes or ambition of the Ashantees, and being opposed to the present, or hitherto so-called, neutrality of the Elminas and others, are determined by every means in their power to obtain the alliance aforesaid.

"That up to the present time your Memorialists have maintained the independence of their allies to the west of the Sweet River; and,

alike to the commerce, civilization, and the political
and general interest of the country, changed at
once the base of operation of the Awoonahs and
Aquamboes, who saw that, if they would continue
the fight, they must do so far in the interior. Sir
Arthur, after remaining eight days at Accra, joined
Captain Glover in the river Volta, convened a
meeting of the contending parties, fully discussed
the disputed point, and on board the colonial
steamer " Eyo," in the river Volta, a treaty of
peace was entered into, on the 30th day of November, 1868, between the representatives of the
Awoonah and Adah nations.

in submission to your Excellency and the officers administering Her
Majesty's Government on the Gold Coast, your Memorialists have
refrained from enforcing their determination of compelling the people
under the Dutch Government to join the alliance, in the hope that
this object may be gained without further bloodshed.

" That your Memorialists submit that a grievous error has been
committed by the high contracting parties to the convention of
March 5, 1867—first, by having failed to consult the people of the
territories to be transferred before the convention was made ; and,
secondly, in exercising coercive measures to enforce the fulfilment
and observance of the convention, when it was known by the officers
exercising such measures that the people were opposed to it.

"Your Memorialists now propose what appear to them the only
way of rectifying the error, and settling the difficulties it has involved, and beg your Excellency to endeavour to carry out their
proposals, which are that negotiations be at once opened for the

It stipulated that the river Volta was to be kept open for all lawful trades ; that the Governor-in-Chief should be umpire in all difference or dispute, whose decision should be final and binding upon both parties ; that the allies be called upon to lay down their arms, and consolidate the peace thus formed.

After the exploration of the river, and when Captain Glover had completed his soundings, they weighed anchor, and left for Lagos. The Aquamboes and Ashantees, the most troublesome of the allies, were not represented in the meeting. About a week

---

purchase of the Dutch settlements on the Gold Coast by Her Majesty's Colonial Government.

" Your Memorialists further submit that the Dutch Government, being at once and for ever debarred from obtaining slaves from Ashantee, will have no object in maintaining their possessions, for your Memorialists are not aware that the commercial relations of the Dutch with their settlements are of any value, and the fact of their decline is patent.

" Your Memorialists now beg your Excellency to endeavour to carry out the prayer of this Memorial, which they consider and believe will relieve their country of its present difficulties, and elevate it to the condition of other dominions of Her Majesty. Otherwise, they fear the whole country will be hopelessly involved in the horrors of war for an indefinite period, to the detriment of Her Majesty's interests as well as those of your Memorialists.

" And your Memorialists, as in duty bound, will ever pray.
" GOLD COAST, WEST AFRICA, November 1868."

after the signing of the treaty, the Aquamboes, with some Ashantee marauders, vigorously attacked Creepee, a flourishing commercial province closely allied to Accra, and committed severe bloodshed. They stopped the navigation of the Volta; the Ashantee army attempted the invasion of the plains of Crobboe; cold-blooded murder, plunder, and all its concomitant mischief continued until February, when the Acting Administrator, Mr. Simpson, landed, on the 15th, at Accra. He held a meeting on the next and following days with the kings, chiefs, and leading merchants, as well as others of the community, who informed him of the continued messages from Akim, Crobboe, Aquapim, Creepee, and Agotins; that the Ashantees had poured large forces into Aquamboe and Creepee, and that they required help from them. On the 24th he left the coast for the disturbed district in the interior, in order to see and judge for himself the real condition of affairs. On the 5th he arrived at Odumassie, in the province of Crobboe, whence he sent for the King of Aquamboe, who flatly refused compliance with his request. He proceeded to Aquamboe himself to meet the king in his own territory. He was at first well received, and both the king and chiefs gave him all assurance that his mission would be successful. Grand palaver meetings were held, where the Acting Administrator, in eloquent and convincing language, expatiated on the blessings and advantages of peace. The king and chiefs apparently became converted or coincided with the truth of his argument, and eagerly signed a treaty of peace drawn up by him. Mr. Simpson immediately wrote a dispatch full of confidence to the Chief Civil Commandant of Accra, to proclaim to the merchants, kings, chiefs, and all the people that peace was established; that the highway to the interior, the Volta, was opened for legitimate trade; that he would be at Addah on the 12th inst., where he would expect to meet the merchants with their merchandize, to accompany him up the Volta as far as Kpong, thus to prove that peace was really established. He at the same time ordered a *puncheon of rum* and *twenty pieces of moree chintzes* as a dash to the kings and chiefs of Aquamboe. The inhabitants of Accra one and all were indignant at the receipt of the proclamation, and lost all confidence in the tact and negotiating power of Mr. Simpson.

Having completed his business with the high dignitaries of Aquamboe, who drank heartily to his health, he informed them that he was now about to return to the coast. They received the message, but quietly informed him that he and his parties were their prisoners. They then called a secret council, and had a prolonged discussion as to the advisability of decapitating the whole of them. The same night they put fire to the low grass hut where he and his party were sleeping; fortunately, however, they escaped unhurt.

About this time there were about 5,000 Ashantee troops at Aquamboe, and Mr. Simpson, either from diplomacy or from common civility, paid marked attention to the general in command. Mr. Simpson was made a state prisoner for five days, and the Aquamboes were determined either to detain him and his party as their prisoners, and send them to Coomassie, or to execute them. The latter determination prevailed in council; but this was opposed and ultimately overruled by the Ashantee General, who said that it was impossible for the Governor of the Gold Coast to travel in such a mean costume and so badly attended, without retinue and without any insignia of power, but that the prisoner before them must be only an adventurer, and in search of something to do. That they had no palaver whatever with any white man, consequently they should allow him to depart. His wise advice, backed as it was with his 5,000 troops, prevailed, and Mr. Simpson was allowed to leave.

These proceedings, my Lord, which might have led to very serious consequences, I consider as sufficiently instructive to men in power, who are very fond of giving great importance to treaties signed by native chiefs. The people of Accra have been systematically abused for always contending that treaties made by each successive Governor and Governor-in-Chief were not worth more than the paper on which they were written, unless backed by a sufficiency of moral force. Whilst the Aquamboes were signing Mr. Simpson's treaty of peace they had, at the very same time, a design on his life; they signed his treaty one day and made him a state prisoner the next. I am obliged to admit that on this coast the French are far superior to us in the making of treaties with the natives. Whilst we bring the chiefs to reason after long palavering and pleasant phraseology, the French bring them to reason at the point of the bayonet; this treaty they respect and keep, the other they laugh at and break.

I have the honour to be, my Lord,

Your Lordship's most obedient Servant,

J. A. B. HORTON, M.D.

LETTER No. VII.*

TO THE RIGHT HON. EARL GRANVILLE, K.G., D.C.L.,
SECRETARY OF STATE FOR THE COLONIES,
&c., &c., &c.

The Castle, Cape Coast,
February 12, 1870.

My Lord,

In the western district of the Gold
Coast affairs with the Dutch territory continued
most unsatisfactory. On the 30th December, 1868,
a party of Dutch soldiers from Elmina attacked
Aggooafful, a village of Fantee, situated about ten
miles from Elmina; they were driven back, the
sergeant in command killed, seven prisoners and
three breech-loading rifles captured, as well as five
women, who were employed as carriers. These
small skirmishes are of very frequent occurrence in
the Fantee villages in close proximity with Elmina.

After the attack of Elmina by the Fantees in
May, 1868, the inhabitants became dissatisfied with
the conduct of their Governor, and were determined

---

* Reference in Dispatch to Sir Arthur Kennedy, No. 126, dated
March 29, 1870. As to future correspondence on the subject, Mr.
Ussher's letter, dated May 1.

to have him recalled. They, therefore, dispatched a deputation to Holland, consisting of one Dutch officer and a native merchant of intelligence, Mr. George Emissang, to give full information to the Minister of the Colonies of the exact state in which they had been placed, and to request adequate assistance from the Dutch Government. Colonel Boers, the Governor, was recalled, and Colonel Nagtglas, who had served out here for a considerable number of years as Dutch Military Officer, and afterwards as Governor, but had retired on a handsome pension, was sent out as a Royal Commissioner with extensive powers.

Immediately after his arrival, about the latter part of May, 1869, a most unfortunate affair occurred, which had a very disastrous effect on the *prestige* of the Dutch on the whole Gold Coast. About this time the Dutch man-of-war "Amstel" anchored off the town of Commendah. A boat, manned by two officers and nine marines, was sent to ply near the shore, take soundings, and endeavour to find out the mouth of a river which was shown in an old chart in the possession of the captain. The boat by some mishap got amongst the breakers, a heavy roller struck her on her beam end and capsized her, the boat was washed ashore, the senior officer and five of the crew were drowned, and the rest escaped.

The Commendahs, on seeing the boat standing ashore from the vessel, were on the alert, and lay in ambush observing their movements, suspecting some mischievous intentions on the part of the ship's crew. They observed the capsize, and on the five men being washed ashore, they opened fire on them, and closing in, fell on them. One of the crew was wounded, and three surrendered without resistance; the fifth foolishly made a bold stand against them, and his fate was sealed by a heavy blow from the butt end of a musket. The Commendahs removed them into the interior, where the wounded man subsequently died. They then sent to the Fantee Confederation to inform them of what had happened, who sent immediate instructions that the prisoners should be treated with great kindness and attention.

Colonel Nagtglas communicated with the Acting Administrator on the circumstances of the case, and asked Mr. Simpson to use his influence with the natives to get the prisoners restored. He imme

diately sent the Acting Collector of Customs and
Mr. James Davies, of Cape Coast, to Quissie Croom,
where they were imprisoned. The Commendahs
refused to deliver them up, and they received
instructions from the Confederation not to deliver
them up unless a sufficient ransom was paid by the
Dutch Government.

The Hon. George Blankson, a native merchant
of Anamaboe, of great influence, and a member of
the Legislative Council, was dispatched to Quissie
Croom, in Commendah Bush, where the unfortunate prisoners were held, as the representative
of the British Government ; and the Fantee Confederation sent Mr. John Hammond and their
Secretary, Mr. George Blankson, junior, to represent them.   A council was held, and the agents of
the Confederation, as well as the principal chiefs
of Commendah, demanded a ransom of 800 ozs.
gold dust, or £3,200 currency ; the British envoy, on
behalf of the Dutch Government, offered them £100
sterling, which they stoutly refused.   After long
palavering and sundry reductions, the Confederation
accepted 300 ozs. gold dust, or £1,200 currency, as
the price of their redemption.   On the guarantee
of the British representative, two of the prisoners

were sent down first, and the other was held as a hostage until the contract should be fulfilled.

Colonel Nagtglas, attended by Captain Le Jeune, his aide-de-camp, came to Cape Coast in person to pay the amount. He travelled by land ; on crossing the Sweet River, when on British ground, he was escorted by 34 soldiers of the 1st West India Regiment, and was received at Cape Coast with the honours due to his high position. The amount was paid to the agents of the Fantee Confederation, the hostage was delivered up ; and after remaining five days, his Excellency and suite embarked on board the " Amsel " war-ship for Elmina amidst the infuriated rage of the οἱ πολλοί.

The prisoners detailed shocking acts of barbarity committed on them by the Commendahs during their imprisonment. They were deprived of their clothes, and made to sleep on straw ; they had their heads shaved as convicts ; the sailor who was killed had his head and hands taken off and carried into the interior as trophies ; the skin of the head was removed and used as a mask over the head and face of the surviving officer. When, however, the Commendahs were enjoined by the Confederation to treat them carefully, they ceased any further molestation. The redemption took place early in July, 1869.

The Fantee Confederation was satisfied with the conduct of the Commendahs, and from the day of the exchange have persistently refused to acknowledge the Dutch flag, and have employed every stratagem to exorcise it from the province of Commendah. The Dutch Government were terribly annoyed at the melancholy circumstances which had caused them so many lives and so much money ; and their subjects were determined at all hazard to expatriate all British Fantees, either by fair or foul means, from the Dutch territory. All the newly-transferred British subjects were regarded with great suspicion, as having some connection with the Fantee Confederation.

One of the districts handed over to the Dutch by the English Government was Dixcove, the most flourishing commercial town of Ahanta. Soon after the Elmina war, one Appah Essrifi, an Elminan, endeavoured to stir up the Dutch inhabitants of Bousnah to demand for the purpose of execution the delivery of all the Fantees of Dixcove. The demand was made, but being refused by the kings and chiefs of Dixcove, this bloodthirsty indi-

vidual went to Wotopoh, a Dutch town in the
neighbourhood of Boutry, where four natives of
Cape Coast had resided peaceably for several years
as agriculturists, caught them, and would have
executed them, were it not for the timely interference of the chiefs, their friends. He, however,
sold the whole of them as slaves.

The last affair at Commendah set the Elminas
and all the Dutch native inhabitants in open hostility against the Dixcoveans, whose only crime
was that they had been English, and were, consequently, suspected of possessing sympathy with the
Fantee Confederation. They, therefore, meditated
the destruction of Dixcove, as its inhabitants
showed, without open demonstration, a decided
antipathy against the Dutch flag.

About the 6th June, 1869, the Elminas residing
at Bousnah, about three miles from Dixcove,
caught a serf (pawn) of the principal native merchant of Dixcove, a native of Cape Coast, who
had gone to a rivulet of the same name (Bousnah)
to fish ; this place was years ago under the Dutch
flag by conquest. They were determined to kill
him, but the Dutch Commandant residing at Dixcove, Mr. Alvarez, being prevailed upon by the

Dixcoveans, reluctantly rescued him from the Bousnahs. They told Mr. Alvarez that the man had done nothing, but, being a Fantee and a British subject, they, in retaliation for what the Commendahs had done, were determined to kill him. Mr. Alvarez, as it is reported, on hearing this, justified their acts, and told them plainly that had they put the pawn to death he would have said nothing to them, but since he was still alive he was bound to give him protection.

On the return of Mr. Alvarez to Dixcove, he held a meeting in the large Palaver Hall, in the fort, with the kings, chiefs, elders, and merchants of Dixcove, and proclaimed an order, wherein he insisted that not any of the inhabitants of or British subjects residing at Dixcove should go to any of the Dutch towns and provinces by which they were surrounded, without wearing a proper insignia that he or she was a Dutch subject—viz., a miniature Dutch flag attached to the end of their cloth, or on some conspicuous part of their dress—without which he, the Commandant, would not be responsible for the lives of the parties who thus left themselves open to be murdered.

Things remained in this disquieting state until

the 12th June, 1869, a week after the Bousnah affair; but rumours were afloat that the Dutch Governor had supplied all the Ahantas, with the exception of the Dixcoveans, with ammunition. On Saturday, the 12th, Mr. Alvarez demanded that all the ammunition in the stores of the merchants, especially Mensah Coomah, a native merchant who had acquired immense wealth during the English rule, should be removed into the fort; but they refused compliance with this strange demand, and the result was the bombardment and destruction of the flourishing little town of Dixcove, formerly English, but now Dutch.

It appears that there was a tacit understanding between the Dutch Commandant and the Ahantas around Dixcove, for, on Monday, the 14th, two days after the refusal of the Dixcoveans to deliver up their ammunition, at eight a.m. the town of Dixcove was invaded by the Bousnahs and other Dutch Ahantas. Mr. Alvarez gave the signal for their advance, by opening fire from his heavy ordnance on the ramparts of the fort upon the town. The Dixcoveans sallied out, and by their impetuous charges checked the progress of the Ahantas, and between five and six o'clock p.m. drove them back.

On their return to the town Mr. Alvarez opened a murderous fire on them, drove them into the bush, cannonaded the respectable houses, set fire to the town, laid it waste, and the next day handed it over to the Dutch soldiers and the Ahanta army to be pillaged and sacked.*

I have the honour to be, my Lord,

Your Lordship's most obedient Servant,

J. A. B. HORTON, M.D.

---

* The following is a faithful account of the position, commercial origin and value, as well as the destruction of Dixcove, published by Mr. A. Swanzy, of London:—

" Dixcove, situated in lat. 5 N., long. 2' 30" W., has long been known to traders as a commercial town, but it is only within the last thirty-five years that its trade has been of any great importance. About the year 1833, my brother, the late Mr. Frank Swanzy, settled at Dixcove, and commenced business with the neighbouring people, largely developing the resources of the district, and increasing the comfort and well-being of the inhabitants. He resided there for about twelve years, and, as commandant and magistrate, succeeded in preserving peace and administering justice with little or no expense to the British Government. In 1845 Mr. Frank Swanzy left Dixcove, and I went to reside there, and for two years carried on business and acted as magistrate, &c., and from that time to June, 1869, the business thus commenced in 1833 has been carried on, to the great benefit of the people, and with profit to myself, all the best houses in Dixcove having been built by my correspondents.

" For certain financial reasons a treaty was entered into between the British and Dutch Governments, by which it was agreed that on the 1st January, 1868, the whole coast line west of Elmina should be transferred to the Dutch flag, and Dixcove, which for over 150 years had been under British protection, was included in the transfer. This treaty was made and carried out without considering the wishes of the natives or the interests of British traders.

" Knowing the difficulty in recovering debts in the Dutch settlements, I resolved in reducing my credits at Dixcove, and established a factory instead. With this object I purchased a house, and my agent placed in charge of my business there a Mr. W. E. Sam, a native of Cape Coast, who had been some time previously in my service. Mr. Sam carried on at Dixcove a large and profitable business, paying large duties to the Dutch Government, and conforming in every respect to the laws and regulations laid down by it.

"Early in June last Mr. Sam heard that an attack on the town of Dixcove was likely to be made by the inhabitants of Bushwa, Boutry, and other Dutch towns, and he consequently wrote to my agent at Cape Coast, Mr. William Cleaver, begging him to come up and take all possible measures to prevent the attack, and save my property. Mr. Cleaver made the contents of this letter known to Colonel Nagtglas, his Netherlands Mâjesty's Commissioner on the Gold Coast, and was assured by him that he need be under no alarm, and that he intended to remove Mr. Alvarez from his post as commander of Dixcove.

" On the 12th June Mr. Alvarez gave orders that all munitions of war should be removed to Dixcove Fort, and Mr. Q. Mensah, the principal native merchant of the place, refused to deliver up his gunpowder to Mr. Alvarez, when the latter said he would send for Bushwa (or Bossnah) people to come and fight against the people of Dixcove ; and on Mr. Mensah's persisting in retaining his gunpowder, Mr. Alvarez sent one of the Dutch landing waiters, in company with Mr. Sam, to tell him that if he did not deliver up his gunpowder he would seek the interference of Bushwa people to compel him to do so. But Mr. Mensah, believing that an attack on Dixcove was imminent, and that munitions of war had been supplied by the Dutch Government to the people of Boutry, &c., refused to give up his only means of defence. Mr. Sam used his utmost efforts to conciliate both parties, offering large security in my name to the commandant (Mr. Alvarez) that Mr. Mensah should not sell or use his gunpowder without the consent of Mr. Alvarez.

" On Sunday, the 13th June, Dixcove was surrounded by Ahanta people, including the people of Bushwa, Boutry, &c., and Mr. Sam used every effort to prevent bloodshed, offering to send large presents to the principal Ahanta chief to conciliate him ; but Mr. Alvarez refused his intercession. On Sunday evening, at a late hour, Mr. Alvarez offered to permit Mr. Sam to remove my property into Dixcove Fort, promising to write to Mr. Sam to that effect on the following morning—a promise which, however, he never fulfilled. Under any circumstances, the offer was too late, as it was impossible to remove my property before the attack commenced; and Mr. Sam distrusted Mr. Alvarez—a distrust showed by the Rev. Mr. Laing, as stated in his affidavit—as the fort was filled with people inimical to Dixcove. Moreover, as my stores were immediately under the fort walls, Mr. Alvarez could have protected my property without removing it had he so desired.

" On Monday morning Mr. Alvarez called at my factory, accompanied by a chief, and told Mr. Sam, in the presence of several witnesses, that all was settled. Mr. Alvarez then had a glass of wine and returned to the fort. In about a quarter of an hour from the time the Commandant left my factory, Dixcove was attacked on all sides; and the Commandant at first positively refused to interfere to prevent the attack, but afterwards agreed to accompany Mr. Sam to the scene of action. When, however, his soldiers refused to go with him, he marched back to the fort. Mr. Sam went alone to the scene of action, and begged the people of Dixcove not to fire, doing all he could to prevent bloodshed.

" The fight commenced about eight o'clock A.M., and during its continuance the guns of Dixcove Fort, placed there for the protection of the town and people, were used for their destruction (the very first shot fired passed through my house and the ball lodged in the piazzi). The guns continued at intervals playing on the town, setting part of it on fire. Whether these guns were fired by the orders of Mr. Alvarez or contrary to them I am unable to say, and I leave the alternative to be appreciated by his superiors. Notwithstanding this disadvantage the Dixcove people kept back their enemies, although trained soldiers, armed with breech-loading rifles, were among the latter; but on the Dixcove people returning to the town about five or six o'clock P.M., the fort guns again were used against them, and, unable to resist such a destructive fire, they retired to the bush about dusk.

"On the following day (Tuesday, the 15th June) the people of Bushwa and Boutry, &c., having no enemies within reach, proceeded to plunder and destroy all the property found in the town; and this was done in the presence of Mr. Alvarez, who states in his affidavit that he told the people not to plunder my property, and I therefore infer that he made no effort to stop the general pillage.

" The value of the property stolen was very great, consisting of palm oil. A large quantity of cotton goods and all the gold on hand were taken from my house, and some portions of my property were carried into the fort.

"The Dutch native troops participated in the plunder; one of my servants, Mr. Isaac Ruhle, a native of Elmina, having actually purchased from a soldier in Dixcove Fort two pieces of cotton goods with my name on them; but on Mr. Ruhle being recognized by a corporal the goods were taken from him.

"Moreover, some cotton goods stolen from Dixcove were landed at Elmina from a canoe (which I believe to have been one of my canoes), and were there taken possession of by Dutch soldiers or constables. Again, Mr. Cleaver informed Colonel Nagtglas that the supercargo of a Dutch vessel, then in Elmina roads, had purchased a considerable quantity of my goods at less than one-third the usual price; and yet Colonel Nagtglas, as far as I know, took no steps to ascertain the fact, but stated that all the plundered property was removed to the bush.

" The iron safe, in which was a large amount in gold dust, was found broken open and empty, close to Dixcove Fort, all my books being also taken away or destroyed.

" Having stated the principal facts connected with this disgraceful outrage—facts which I believe can be completely substantiated— I feel sure the Government of his Majesty the King of the Netherlands will, without delay, institute a strict inquiry into all the circumstances attending it, and after making due reparation for losses already sustained, will take measures to prevent any repetition of such wholesale destruction of life and property in their Gold Coast settlements.

" A. SWANZY.

" 122, Cannon-street, London, Sept. 30, 1869."

LETTER No. VIII.

TO THE RIGHT HON. EARL GRANVILLE, K.G., D.C.L.,
SECRETARY OF STATE FOR THE COLONIES,
&c., &c., &c.

THE CASTLE, CAPE COAST,
March 12, 1870.

MY LORD,

The bombardment and destruction of
Dixcove was by no means a happy event for the inhabitants of the whole Gold Coast, inasmuch as it
created a feeling of universal distrust in the breast
of every individual member of the Gold Coast Protectorate, and confirmed the opinion which they had
formed of the pernicious effects of the transfer of
territory, and the handing over of subjects attached
to the flag of England by tradition and universal
appreciation and predilection to the Dutch, with
whom they can never be reconciled.

Just before this bombardment, on the 12th June,
1869, Captain Pieter Willen Alvarez, Dutch Commandant, went round the town of Dixcove, with
armed soldiers, and took an account of all the gunpowder in the merchants' stores, and placed a guard
upon every house supposed to contain it. The mer-

chants having refused to deliver over to him their munitions of war, Captain Alvarez, who evidently was in league with the Ahantas, destroyed the town.

The people of Dixcove, who have had a filial regard for the British Government, rushed down to Government House at Cape Coast, and laid their complaints to the Administrator, requesting him to interfere and compel the Dutch Government to give them ample redress for the losses they had sustained. The factory of Messrs. F. and A. Swanzy was broken into (*vide* Appendix No. 2), and property to the amount of £7,998 9s. 7d., for which he claims compensation, stolen. His Excellency Governor Nagtglas accounted for the supply of ammunition to the Ahantas around Dixcove from information which he had received that King Affo, in command of the Wassaws, had intended to invade their territory (Dutch Ahanta), and that they were to be assisted by the inhabitants of Dixcove. He expressed his surprise that, during the attack of Dixcove by the Ahantas, assisted by the Dutch regular forces from the fort of Boutry (who were armed with breech-loading rifles), and the bombardment by the Fort, the Wassaws did not come to the assistance of the Dixcoveans. Adequate measures were not, however, taken to prove whether these rumours were based on fact before this ruthless destruction of life and property took place.

Whilst these proceedings were going on along the sea-coast, a movement which will remain immortal in the annals of the Gold Coast was being prosecuted at Coomassie, the capital of Ashantee. At the death of Quacoe Duah, late King of Ashantee, messengers were sent to all the allies of the kingdom to inform them of the fact, and each messenger, as he delivered the awful news, was quickly dispatched into the unknown world to attend upon the deceased monarch. In this case a message was sent to the King of Elmina, who received the mournful news with great lamentation, and dispatched the unfortunate teller to the region of spirits. Soon afterwards he sent one of his chiefs, Andor by name, to the Court of Coomassie to condole with the nation for their loss, and to assist in the funeral obsequies. After completing his mission, the present King of Ashantee sent him back escorted by several hundred armed men, under command of Chief Atjiempon, the brother of the late king, by route of Aöwen (Awowen), with a message to the king of that place to permit them to pass through his territory. After passing through Aöwen, one of the chiefs of the Amantiful territory detained him for nearly four months. A great many of the camp followers returned. From Amantiful they marched to Asinee, and the French Government permitted Atjiempon, with three hundred of his followers, to cross over the river Asinee to Appolonia. At Appolonia Atjiempon seems not to have taken that reckless and bloody fit which marked his further progress through the Dutch Territory on the Gold Coast. Leaving Appolonia, one of the newly-transferred provinces, he proceeded to Axein, a province which has ever belonged to the Dutch. His first act, through the instigation of Andor, the Elminan, was to cut off the tongue of a Fantee resident, and subsequently his head, in the market place, about 300 yards from the Dutch fort.

After this, wherever he came, he decapitated every Fantee who might chance to fall into his hands, so that his name carried terror and consternation to the breast of every Fantee resident in the Dutch Territory, and they were to be seen flying helter-skelter from the sea-coast into the interior provinces of Wassaw and Denkera to escape the dreadful knife of the executioner.

On the 14th November, Mr. Cleaver, agent for
Messrs. F. and A. Swanzy, merchants, and Captain
Dale of the merchant brig " Alligator," landed at
Axein for the purpose of trading with the natives as
the former had oftentimes done. Atjiempon with
the King of Axein were determined to make them
prisoners, cut off their heads, or compel their
principal to pay a heavy ransom for them ; but the
firmness of the Dutch Commandant, who it might
be worthy of notice had English blood in him,
coupled with the resolute stand made by Mr.
Cleaver, prevented the carrying into effect their
mischievous intention.   For let it be said that
Atjiempon, before he left Coomassie, took an oath
to kill any Englishman he might meet with.

During his bloody march through the sea-coast,
he killed several of the Fantees whom he
chanced to meet in the towns and villages, and at
Tancoorah two became victims of his atrocities.
At Secondee, where there is a Dutch fort under
command of a Dutch officer, seven of the Fantee
residents, who had for years resided in English and
Dutch Secondee, and formed connexions there, took
refuge in the fort, and claimed the protection of
the Dutch flag from the cynical butchery of the

bloodthirsty chief. On the arrival of Atjiempon, he demanded that the men should be given up, and accompanied his demand with force, and ultimately compelled the Dutch Commandant to deliver them up to him for the express purpose of putting them to death. And would it be believed that the Dutch Commandant actually delivered these poor victims to the ruthless hands of the Ashantee? I would cry *credo quia impossibile est,* were I not in possession of sufficient testimony on oath to corroborate every tittle of the statement.*

---

* Statement of the Ashantee captive, Government House, 13th January, 1870.—The Chiefs of Cape Coast, Mr. Blankson, and others, present. Quacoe Adjapon, captured by the Fantees at Agoonah, and ransomed by the Government, came down with Andor (Dutch messenger) and Atjiempon from Coomassie. It is about nine months or nearly a year since he left. He came though Amantiful's Territory, and was detained by · him at Kunjaboe for four months. A great many Ashantees who had come went back. When they (Atjiempon's party) came to Axein, they saw the white men from the ship. Atjiempon wanted to kill them, but the Dutch Commandant would not let them, but had great difficulty in preventing them. At Appolonia they did not molest the Fantees, but at Axein, Andor (the Elmina messenger) told Atjiempon to kill the Fantees there. He accordingly killed one, and put one in log. He did the same at every place till he came to Secondee. Previous to their arrival at Secondee, he killed two at Tancoorah (Taccorary) Seven Fantees were given up to Atjiempon at Secondee. They were in the Dutch fort; so he demanded them from the Commandant, who eventually gave them up to him, and he killed two of them.

This Atjiempon—this *rara avis in terris Hollandis*—used the executioner's knife over the neck of two or three of these prisoners, besides two other natives of Cape Coast—viz., Enkookoo, whose nose was first cut off and his jaw-bone carried on his horn and his skull on his drum, and an aged man by the name of Reynold, who escaped the horrible ordeal of torture before being murdered. The rest of the men escaped this awful fate through the remonstrance of Colonel Nagtglas, the Dutch Governor.

The news of Atjiempon's bloody march preceded him to Elmina, and his approach was a signal for a general decampment from that place of all its Fantee residents, even those who had taken up arms with the Elminas against their *confrères* of the same nationality. At Elmina itself—where stand strong fortifications, bristling with five muzzle and breech-loading heavy cannons ; where Dutch marines and Batavian regulars, with their improved rifles, in vast numbers, occupy every stronghold of the town ;

At Secondee, the Commandant wrote to the Governor, who remonstrated with Atjiempon, and requested him to bring the rest to Elmina, which he did.

Before me, H. T. USSHER, Administrator.

where two men-of-war at her roadstead ride at
anchor with their broadsides commanding every portion of the town—even here Atjiempon's atrocious
acts, and the voice of the dead and dying, cry loudly
for vengeance against the civilized government of
Holland.*

---

* The following is an account of an attempt on the life of Mr.
W. C. Finlason, of Cape Coast, a creole of Jamaica (white), who
visited Elmina early this year :—

"Hamilton House, Cape Coast, March 26, 1870.

"My dear Horton,—In conformity with your request of this
date, I send you the following account of the cowardly attack made
on me by the ignorant King of Elmina, aided by the barbarous and
cruel captain of Ashantee, named Atjiempon, on the night of the
12th instant, whilst on a visit to Elmina, by invitation of Mr.
George E. Eminsang, a member of the Dutch Legislative Council
at that place.

"I left Cape Coast on the 11th instant by the British barque
'Albert' (Captain Webber). On the 12th we arrived at Elmina,
and about four o'clock P.M. I landed, and proceeded to Mr.
Eminsang's hotel. After dinner I proposed to Captain Webber
and Mr. Eminsang that we should go for a walk ; and just as we
were going out a lot of the King of Elmina's people rushed in, and
wanted to know what I was doing in Elmina, and desired that I
should go to the king's house. Mr. Eminsang, *unauthorized* by me,
told the messengers that we were going for a walk, and, as it was
moonlight, we would call in and see the king if possible. We then
proceeded on our walk about eight o'clock P.M. The first house I
visited was the Hon. Mr. Molenar's. After being there a quarter of
an hour we proceeded to Mrs. Charlotte Bartels', one of the most
respectable ladies of Elmina. We had not been there half an hour
before the same men who came to Mr. Eminsang's rushed in, and

Quabina Otoo, a native of Sraffah, in British Fantee, stated amongst other things before the Administrator of the Gold Coast, Mr. Ussher, and the chiefs and captains of Cape Coast, on the 10th January last, that six of them (Fantees) were re-

---

asked Mr. Eminsang why I had not come to the king's house. Mr. Eminsang offered some explanation, which did not seem to please the men, and they went away. In ten minutes they returned, with an imperative order for me to proceed to the king's house at once, and dared me to refuse at my peril. I did refuse; and told them that I was a white man, and, what was more, I was not a Fantee, and consequently I would obey no one but the Governor of Elmina. This message, I presume, was taken to the King of Elmina, who, in less than half an hour, rushed into Mrs. Bartels' house with all his people, and after a few moments' silence commenced to accuse me of writing against the Elminas in the *African Times*, and also with being secretary to the Fantee Confederation at Mankessim, and consequently I was an enemy to the Elminas, and that I only came there to act as a spy against them. I indignantly repudiated the whole of his accusations, and assured him he was in error, and that I never once wrote against him or his people; that all I ever wrote was in their favour. He then gave me the lie, and accompanied it with a lot of low vulgar Fantee abuse. I then considered it expedient to treat all he said with contempt. At this time the people began to gather in hundreds round the house, and at the hour of twelve o'clock at night a drum was sounded, which was the signal for a general burst of yelling and weeping by Mrs. Bartels and all her people. I inquired what was the reason of all this, when I was told that the Ashantee captain's death-drum had sounded, and that was the signal for me to lose my head. My friend Captain Webber, who was with me, got into a fearful state of excitement; and I immediately took off my watch and chain and handed it to him to keep, so that I might at least have a fight

siding at Adjuapenin, a village in close proximity to Elmina, and when they heard of Atjiempon's approach, they endeavoured to make their escape to Cape Coast in three canoes. They were chased by two canoes from Elmina; they captured the canoe

---

before parting with that most necessary part of my body. In a few moments I saw a young, handsome fellow with a knife and a bludgeon. This was the executioner; and I got up from my chair as he advanced to me, and, holding a good-sized stick in my hand, I defied him to advance. During this critical moment, when all hope seemed to have fled, the bugle sounded, and in an instant a Dutch officer stepped in the hall, with his drawn sword, and called out for me. I immediately made my exit from the savage King of Elmina and his bloody friend Atjiempon, who appeared perfectly dumbfounded at my sudden release. Immediately on my going to the bottom of the steps I found 150 soldiers with fixed bayonets ready to escort me to the fort, which I reached about half-past twelve o'clock. I was taken to the Secretary, Major Le Jeune, who most kindly and hospitably entertained me. The next day the Governor told me I could leave Elmina at ten o'clock if I liked, and that he would give me an escort to the landing-place. I gladly accepted his Excellency's kind offer, and accordingly, under an escort of 200 soldiers, I was taken to the landing-place, and escorted by Captain Alvarez, a Dutch officer, on board the 'Albert' in the Government boat. On the 16th the Commodore of the Dutch man-of-war 'Koopman' took me to Cape Coast, where I landed, feeling indeed grateful to an overruling Providence for the narrow escape I had met with. Mrs. Bartels' great influence kept these savage wretches from carrying out their bloody deed for nearly an hour. To her and the Governor and the officers of Elmina I owe a deep debt of gratitude.—Yours sincerely,

"WM. CHAS. FINLASON."

in which he was, the others, however, escaped. His
uncle was killed in cold blood, and his head was
brought and placed in his hand; his mother was
beaten with clubs to death. It was determined by
Atjiempon that he should be killed, but fortunately
for him he slipped off the log which secured his
hand, and made his escape into the bush. This was
not an isolated case at this time, as many of the
Fantees were beaten to death with clubs at Elmina.

Complaints were every day brought to the Administrator of the English Gold Coast by relatives
of those who had been murdered in cold blood, and
the kings and chiefs complained most bitterly of the
conduct of the Dutch Government and the Elminans, so that Mr. Ussher dispatched a letter to his
Excellency Colonel Nagtglas, enclosing copies of all
the affidavits and declarations made before himself
and other justices of the peace of the settlement
relative to the murders which had been committed
on British subjects or persons under British protection in Dutch territory, and also the infamous
.march of Atjiempon from Appolonia to Elmina;
and expressed hopes that his Excellency would inflict
condign punishment upon the Ashantee chieftain and
his people, as a warning to others attempting to ac

in a similar manner. He informed him that at Cape
Coast he saw the Dutch sergeant of police walking
freely, unarmed, in the most crowded portion of the
town without molestation ; that at present several
persons, natives of Elmina, were residing at Cape
Coast, and when from the conduct of the Elminans
on their countrymen attempts were made to molest
them, prompt and efficient measures were used to
repress it ; that early in 1868, when the Fantees
took up arms against Elmina, Quassie Ferocoo was
murdered by his own brother Cromantines* for refusing to go to war against Elmina ; that he, the
Administrator, dispatched a large force to that
place, seized the perpetrators of the act, and sen-
tenced them to severe punishment from the king
downwards ; that at this present moment there were
at Cape Coast 30 Ashantees, who walk about the
town unmolested and happy.

Colonel Nagtglas was indignant with Atjiempon
for his unwarranted conduct towards the peaceful
Fantee residents in the Dutch territory, and refused
to grant him audience ;—but for only a few days; for

---

* The Cromantines were people lately transferred from the
Dutch to the English rule.

such is the desire of keeping up friendly relations with the arbitrary potentate at Coomassie that nothing further was done to him. He enjoyed and is still enjoying unlimited liberty and licence at Elmina.

My Lord, the question now arises—What has been the result of the convention for the exchange of territory between the English and the Dutch Governments on the Gold Coast ?

1st. It has led to a vast increase of the revenue of the two Governments ; and whilst the expenditure of the English on their officials has not materially been increased, that of the Dutch has been increased tenfold.

2nd. It has established a compact Government along the sea-coast of the British possession ; but a state of disquietude, unhappiness, disruption, and unsettled government in the Dutch sea-board towns.

3rd. It has led to the formation of a CONFEDERATION of all the kings of the interior of the British Protectorate for social improvement and mutual support, offensive and defensive, loyal to the Government of the sea-coast.   In the Dutch interior, a defiance and hatred of the Dutch rule by the interior tribes (Wassaws and Denkeras) who have just been transferred ; a readiness to take up arms against the Dutch ; a state of feverish excitement and uncertainty as to their future condition, and the formation of an alliance with the Fantee Confederation, offensive and defensive, against the Dutch and the Ashantees.

4th. It has produced peace, quietness, and prosperity in all the towns handed over by the Dutch to the English rule ; but insurrection, followed by bombardment and destruction, of the important and flourishing towns handed over to the Dutch.

5th. It has afforded protection to the Elminas and Ashantees residing at Cape Coast and other parts under British rule ; but led to cold-blooded murder of the Fantees who had made Elmina their home, as well as those who had intended to end their days in British Ahanta, now transferred to Dutch rule.

6th. It has led to a future of perpetual disruption and loss of influence over the potentate at Coomassie by the British authority ; it has brought that potentate and the Dutch Government into a closer union and a more friendly relationship.

I have the honour to be,

Your Lordship's most obedient Servant,

J. A. B. HORTON, M.D.

LETTER No. IX.

TO THE RIGHT HON. EARL GRANVILLE, K.G., D.C.L., SECRETARY OF STATE FOR THE COLONIES, &c., &c., &c.

CAPE COAST CASTLE,
May 2, 1870.

MY LORD,

As this will be my concluding letter on the affairs of the Gold Coast Settlement, it is necessary that I should give you a birds'-eye view description of the exact state of this settlement, and its relation with surrounding independent tribes.

At the western boundary of the Gold Coast, on the borders of Asinee, there are at present 5,000 armed men from the King of Ashantee imploring in vain the French Government for passage through that country to the Dutch provinces on the sea-coast. Appolonia, which at the time of the transfer was partly in favour of the Dutch Government and partly against it (*vide* Letter I.), is now suffering from the ravages of a civil war. The Bainyeans, who refused to accept the Dutch flag at the very commencement, and whose town was bombarded by the Dutch ship-of-war, have called to their assistance the King of Wassaw, and several engagements have taken place between them and the Attawaboans ; the cry of the combined army being to plant again the British flag in the whole of the province of Appolonia. The Dutch Commandant of Appolonia has deserted the place, removed his men and stores, handed over the key of the fort to the King of Attawaboe, and marched to• Axim, leaving the natives to settle their dispute in the best way they can. Axim and Ahanta, with the exception of Dixcove, which was so recently bombarded, and now reduced to extremities, are for the Dutch. The Wassaws, Chufuls, and Denkeras, interior tribes, have not accepted the Dutch flag, and repudiate the treaty placing them under Dutch rule. The Commendahs are still in open hostilities with the Dutch ; although driven into the interior they continue a guerilla warfare with them. At Elmina things are in a most unsatisfactory state ; that bloody Ashantee chieftain, Atjiempon, has committed outrageous murders on peaceful inhabitants without any assignable cause.* The Elminas, influenced by Atjiempon, crossed the Sweet River (boundary line

---

* The murder of Mr. Emissang's serf in the neighbourhood of Elmina.

between British and Dutch territory), made a raid
on Fantee territory, attacked, pillaged, and burnt to
the ground a Cape Coast village, and marched to
within three and a half miles of Cape Coast Town,
and then retired. The whole of the Fantee tribes
are loyal to the British Government, but, seeing
that the Coast Government has done nothing
towards their social and physical improvement, they
have united in forming a government of their own,
subject, however, to the orders of the British
authority on the sea-coast. The provinces comprise
Assim, Abrah, or Abakrampah, Inguah, Anamaboe,
Mankessim, Ajimacoo, Dominassie, Akumfie, Akim
(eastern and western), and Goomoor. The inhabitants of Cape Coast and Moree are now
encamped on the borders of the Sweet River, with
the object of preventing a similar raid on Fantee
land.

In the eastern, or Accra district of the Gold
Coast, affairs are even worse than in the western.
The combined army of Ashantees, Aquapims, and
Awoonahs, have made themselves masters of the
passes of the river Volta, and have entirely stopped
trade through that channel. The indefatigable
native general, Domprey, has kept them in check,

and prevented them from becoming masters of the western bank. Last month a convoy, composed of ninety-five men, sent with ammunition to him, fell into an ambuscade ; they were attacked and almost cut to pieces. The whole of the people in the Accra district are now on the move to the Volta. His Excellency the Administrator, H. T. Ussher, Esq., left Cape Coast on the 25th April for the disturbed district, in one of the Lagos colonial steamers. He intends to ascend the river Volta, accompanied by a few of the Lagos Housa irregulars and thirteen rank and file of the 1st West India Regiment. He will endeavour to bring the refractory chiefs to reason either by conciliatory measures or, if neces- sary, by the use of force, and show them that he is determined to open up that great artery to the interior of the Gold Coast, the river Volta, and to maintain in her a steamer for the protection of commerce.

There are a few subjects connected with the government of the Gold Coast which I will take the liberty of bringing before your lordship, and the proper consideration of which will tend to establish that peace and concord on the whole of this Coast, which is so necessary for its development and im-

provement. These I will consider under five heads,
—viz.: I. The Administratorship of the Gold Coast;
II. The Settlement of the Dutch Question; III.
Improvement in the Educational Department ; IV.
The Gold Coast Militia; V. The Fantee Con-
federation.

I. The Administratorship of the Gold Coast.

Unlike all the other Governments on the Western Coast of Africa, that of the Gold Coast is influenced by many surrounding circumstances which
make it the most difficult of them all, and require
great tact and magnanimity in the executive. Its
close proximity to the settlement of a very small
European Power, whose policy of government is
totally different from that of the British ; its position on the sea-coast, in front of a powerful potentate, who has a compact Government, and who
regards the people under British Protectorate with
hatred ; its commerce being almost wholly dependent on that interior tribe- -the Ashantees—who
are always at war with them, and who consequently
have the power of putting a check to the wants and
requirements of the commercial population on
the British territory; its inhabitants, claiming

British protection, but disclaiming themselves as British subjects, each regarding himself as an independent individual in alliance with the British Government ;—these circumstances make the Gold Coast by no means an easy Government. Besides, the extent of country is so large, the views and wishes of the people in each province so different, the difficulty of access to the country so great, the orders for non-intervention which the Administrators are constantly receiving from the Home Authorities are so general, and matters of importance within the Protectorate are so frequently arising requiring prompt, decisive, and immediate action, that it is no wonder that the Gold Coast Government is considered by men of experience as a trying ordeal for one who is appointed to fill the important post of head of the executive there.

The Governor or Administrator of the Gold Coast should be a man of tact, resolution, and great independence. Whilst firm in his decision, which should only be arrived at after matured consideration, he should be most magnanimous and conciliatory to the inhabitants over whom he exercises supreme authority. He should be a man who, by long experience in the manners, customs, and habits of the peculiar people of this coast, could form an adequate judgment as to the measures necessary to avert internal disturbance, and to give them a generalized conception of the interest the Home Government has always manifested, and will still continue to manifest, towards their advancement.   He should be an official Nelson ; not a pedantic martinet, but one who would dare to disobey from a paramount sense of duty.

I verily believe, my Lord, that in the government of a semi-barbarous race, where the aim is to bring up the governed rapidly to advancement in industrial pursuits, education, and general social condition, *a little despotism is absolutely necessary.* But it must be understood that this despotism must not be used for the exertion of uncalled-for arbitrary power, which an intelligent race might think, simply from its superior intelligence, it ought to exact over the other as being less informed.   But it should be more on principles of equity, having this object in view—the *material advancement of the people.*   It will, however, be a most deplorable thing for any Government if this little despotism is exercised for revenge, or for the purpose of satisfying private pique.

II. The Settlement of the Dutch Question.

Events have now taken such a fearful turn in the Government of the Gold Coast, that nothing but a complete transformation of the mode of governing the Dutch territory can lead to a happy conclusion of the difficulties hanging over the political atmosphere of the settlement. Every day the difficulties of the question become more and more apparent. The insubordination of even the Elminas to the direct commands of the Dutch Government, or their tardy obedience to its rule ; the atrocities of the few Ashantees who have found their way into the Dutch capital, unparalleled in the civilized history of the Gold Coast ; and the enormous expenditure which the Dutch Government at the Hague are, through the unsettled state of the country, bound to keep up —are sufficient *à priori* arguments to prove that the present state of the Gold Coast politics is untenable.

There are two courses opened to the Dutch Government—viz. :—

First—To declare against Ashantee, and induce their subjects to enter into an alliance with the Fantee, offensive and defensive.

Second—To get rid of their possessions in the best possible way.

It is not likely that the Dutch Government nor their subjects would break up their alliance with Ashantee, which from time immemorial has been cemented through various phases of struggles which the Ashantees have had with the Coast tribes. The Dutch Fantees or Ashantees would rather maintain the *statu quo* as long as they are under the Dutch flag : the first course is consequently not easily admissible.

The second course is the only one by which the Dutch will be able to close their affairs on this coast honourably. They may come to terms for the sale of their possessions either to the English, French, or North German Confederation. If sold to the English, we shall have under command the whole of the Gold Coast, with the exception of a small portion to the westward, now occupied by the French ; and, with the judicious supply of custom officers, the revenue will be vastly increased, so that from being now between £20,000 to £30,000 a year, we can safely reckon, when trade in the interior is opened, on from £70,000 to £100,000. We shall then be able to bring the Ashantees to terms more easily and readily than before. But the material advancement of the Coast would be exceedingly slow ; the field would be too large for the means of improvement at the Administrator's command, a scattered machinery would most likely be put to work, and the result would be unsatisfactory.

If sold to the French, they would have a continuous possession from Assinee to the Sweet River, a country of unknown mineral wealth. They would disdain to uphold the pretensions of Ashantee; and such is my knowledge of them in the Senegambia, that I most assuredly believe they would quickly form an alliance with our Government against any native Government, and would put down within a very short time the waywardness of the Elminas. The Wassaws and Denkeras would submit to their dictation, they would open roads into the interior to the boundary of Ashantee, and the capital of Ashantee—Coomassie—would soon fall into their hands. They would improve the country and people, make good Catholics of the latter, put down their barbarous customs, and teach them the mechanical arts. Indeed their occupation, if measured by the improvements accomplished by them at Daka, near Goree, only lately annexed by the French Government, would be of immense advantage to the Gold Coast.

If sold to the North German Confederation there will be three powers within a coast line of only 300 miles (as it at present is), whose interests would differ greatly. The Germans are a hard-working plodding race. Whilst they would have very little to do with Ashantee, they would not join so readily with the English as the French would to oppose them. Not being a colonizing Government, their measures would be experimental ; the interior tribes would not take very easily with them ; they would, however, develop the resources of the interior, the gold mines of Wassaw and Denkera would be profitably worked, and there would be a great number of German emigrants, which would be of great advantage to the country.

III. Improvement in the Educational Department.

The greatest want on the Gold Coast is proper educational establishments; the present schools are lamentably deficient, and it is of the greatest importance to know that the subject has the sympathy of the Administrator,* who has now set on foot

---

* Letter from Dr. Horton to H. T. Ussher, Esq., Administrator, with reply :—

My dear Governor,—Permit me to offer you my sincere thanks

certain measures by which the standard can be greatly improved. His Excellency has requested the Rev. Thos. Maxwell, Acting Colonial Chaplain, and myself, to draw up a scheme for establishing a good school on the Gold Coast, calculated to afford encouragement to the Fantees for sending their children for education there, and the following scheme will be laid before him on his return from his trip on the Volta, viz. :—

1. That a Government Day School be organized in each of the four principal seaport towns—viz., Cape Coast, Anamaboe, Winnebah, and Accra.

2. That an Academy be formed at Cape Coast, under the auspices of the Government, for the more advanced pupils, who should be drafted from the Day Schools, and that the Academy be opened to the public.

3. That well-trained teachers or schoolmasters be secured, after due examination, from the Gold Coast, Sierre Leone, or elsewhere, who should be liberally paid by the Government.

4. That the Principal of the Academy be a man

---

for the liberal subscription you have made for yourself and for the Government over which you preside on behalf of the work which I am about to publish. This leads me to bring to your Excellency's

who has had experience in the training and bringing up of youths, and that his salary be from £200 to £250 a-year.

5. That the Academy be made to furnish efficient schoolmasters for the outposts in the Protectorate.

6. That a Board of Education, composed of Government officials and merchants, be formed, any member of which Board should visit the School at any time, and report in a book, kept for that purpose, the condition of the School.

7. That in the Day Schools the principal studies

---

notice certain recommendations, which I have long ago considered will meet with your approbation, relative to certain improvements in one of the most important branches of this Government—I mean the Educational Department. There is at present in the Grammar School at Freetown, Sierra Leone, a native tutor who was educated in England, and who is well conversant with the approved method of teaching. He has a general knowledge of the rudimentary studies necessary for bringing up young persons, as well as of Greek, Latin, and mathematics. I have been speaking to the Rev. Thos. Maxwell relative to the lamentable state of the schools here, which is mainly due to the want of efficient schoolmasters, and he spoke very highly of this tutor, Mr. Bowen, who he also said would be glad to exchange his present position for another more advantageous and lucrative. His companion, whilst in England, a Mr. Kates, is now Government schoolmaster at the Gambia, employed by Major Braoo, the Administrator; and I think, if your Excellency would consider the suggestion worthy of the good of the country, the services of Mr. Bowen can be secured to commence a

taught should be English grammar, arithmetic, reading, spelling, geography, writing, and dictation.

8. That in the Higher School the subjects for education should include, besides grammar and geography, the rudiments of Latin and Greek, Euclid, geometry, botany, mineralogy, and music.

9. That there should be appointed an Inspector of Schools, who should report once or twice a-year as to the condition of each School. That the Administrator instruct the Commandant of each

---

substantial Government school here, under the superintendence of the chaplain of the colony.—I am, &c.,

AFRICANUS HORTON.

REPLY.]

Government House, April 21, 1870.

My dear Dr. Horton,—The subject of schools is one that has long had my sympathy. Although I am the head of the Executive here, no one knows and recognizes better than myself the very low standard existing here in that respect. I had a long talk with Mr. Maxwell on the subject. I propose introducing into the estimates for 1871 a large grant towards educational purposes, certainly not less than 1,000l. to begin with, and more if requisite. I have asked the Acting Colonial Chaplain to furnish me, on my return from the Volta, with full suggestions as to the best scheme for establishing a good school here, which should be of a higher class than hitherto, and also calculated to afford encouragement to the Fantees to send their children. If during my absence you would like to talk to Mr. Maxwell and draw up a scheme with him, it shall receive my best attention.—Very truly yours,   H. T. USSHER.

district to have a general supervision over the Schools in his command.

10. That there be two Sessions for the Academy and Day Schools, one to commence on the first Monday in July and terminate on the second Monday in December, and the other to commence on the third Monday in January, and terminate on the first Monday in June.

11. That at the termination of each Session a public examination should be held in all the Schools, that of the Day Schools in *viva voce*, under the superintendence of the Civil Commandant of the District, and that of the Academy in writing and *viva voce*, and that the public be invited to attend.

I have no doubt that these propositions will meet with the attention and support of Mr. Ussher, and, if effectually carried out, a glorious future awaits this special department of the Gold Coast Government.

IV. The Gold Coast Militia.

Rumours are afloat that within a very short period of time, the troops serving on the Gold Coast would be indefinitely withdrawn; and Mr. Cardwell's speech of March 3rd, in the House of Commons, in explanation of the reduction in the

military forces in general, and the 3rd West India
Regiment in particular, stated that the present
Governor-in-Chief, whilst in England in October
last, informed your Lordship and himself that
" what two regiments could not do five years ago,
two companies were able to do at present, and that
but for a temporary interruption of tranquillity
between the Dutch and some blacks in the neighbourhood of the Gold Coast, he would have been
perfectly content with those two companies only at
Sierra Leone." There is, therefore, a very great
presumptive reason to suppose that, should the
Dutch difficulties be removed, the troops would be
withdrawn entirely from the Gold Coast.

At present the Administrator's hands are so tied
down, that the military are an expensive ornament
to him, because their movements, for even defensive
purposes, are accompanied with so many respon-
sibilities, that their assistance was scarcely ever
asked for in cases of disturbances not within the
precincts of the barracks ; so that a good native
force, under the pay of the Colonial Government
(local) and command of the Administrator, will be
of more service to him. It is true that the troops
bring a large quantity of cash to the country, and

act as a check to any offensive movement by the
native tribes on the Government of the sea-coast,
but for all other purposes they are of very little use
to the colony.

The Local Government ought now to be on the
alert, and commence to embody and train up a
number of men who would form the Gold Coast
Militia, to replace the troops whenever the time for
their withdrawal shall arrive. It is at present under
contemplation to enlist a number of Lagos Housas
to serve on the Gold Coast. Without doubt, those
Housas which are met with in the Lagos irregular
force are a fine and trustworthy body of men
They require to be treated with scrupulous care and
attention before they can agree to serve as soldiers ;
and as a local corps on the Gold Coast, where the
living and habits of the people are very different
from what they are accustomed to, unless they are
very much attached to the person of the Administrator, they would be found to be insubordinate and
useless, and would entail great trouble and expense
to the local authority.

The Gold Coast Militia, to answer the purposes
for which they would be enlisted, must be composed
of free Fantees. The Administrator should obtain

ten or more picked men from every province of the
Gold Coast under the Protectorate, who should be
liberally treated; not be kept to strict military
discipline, but allowed greater liberties. They
should be drilled in Fantee, officered by Europeans
and natives, and taught bush fighting. When this
is accomplished, the Administrator can with ease
dispense with the services of the troops.

V. THE FANTEE CONFEDERATION.

The political constitution of the interior tribes on
the Gold Coast is of a very primitive order, and
their social organization resembles most closely the
feudal system of Europe in the middle ages. A
king is acknowledged, who in former years exercised
the most unbounded authority as feudal lord, retaining paramount right or *dominicum directum*
over the life and property of all the wealthiest
nobles or caboceers of his kingdom. Under the
kings are powerful chiefs (barons) and princes of the
blood, who exercise considerable authority over their
vassals, levy taxes, command a division (cohort) of
the army, undertake distant expeditions, receiving
under their protection inferior chiefs or free families
who are wealthy, but who do not possess sufficient

numbers of vassals to protect themselves from the influences of neighbouring powerful caboceers or chiefs. These families consent to hold their property and estate as their feudatories, and may be regarded as the *inferior nobility* of the ancient feudal states. Then come the free inhabitants, who, although not wealthy, have considerable influence in the country; these people are dependent on or claim vassalage to powerful feudal caboceers for protection. Then come the real vassals or serfs (*villicus*), who cultivate the land, and who are generally slaves received into the inheritance of a feudal caboceer (baron) or their vassals.

Before the English became influential on the Gold Coast, this feudal system was carried on to a very high degree. The feudal kingdoms were conglomerations of many heterogeneous states, who acknowledged a king as their feudal lord, and he, on his part, was to a considerable extent a vassal of the powerful King of Ashantee. But since the English Government has had a complete hold on the sea-coast towns, and made the feudal lords or kings independent of the Ashantee potentate, as well as since it has exercised considerable influence over the institutions of each feudal kingdom, a universal spirit of disaffection and sedition reigns in the interior; the influence of each regal Government has declined in a very considerable degree; each feudal-baron or chief, according to his strength, power, and audacity, finding that he is not dependent on the king or feudal lord, but the kings on him, according to the number of vassals under his command, pays but very little attention to his orders, in many cases, in fact, defying him openly. In many places the king is deprived of all regal power, and his retinue or *comitatus* is of the poorest order, and even the external honour of royalty is but meagrely accorded him. Internal convulsions without much violence are not unfrequent; and now a state of agitation exists in the interior; the feudal system is tottering to its foundation; a more enlightened Government is earnestly demanded by even the nominal feudal lords or kings and the wealthy caboceers (barons) and people. But the people are most woefully deficient in the two essential elements of real liberty and the means of having a settled order of things— viz., *education* and *industry.*

If the Government of the interior tribes is to be continued in the very unsatisfactory and undefined manner in which it has been carried on for the last century by the Government on the coast, it will take more than three hundred years to bring it to that state of political civilization which will fit them for independence after fully shaking off the yoke of their feudal lords. And I hazard the opinion, my Lord, that if the regeneration and civilization of the fine race of interior tribes is to be left to the present system of Coast Government, it will certainly take another hundred years to infuse only the germ of civilization amongst them and to enlighten them in the true principles of a civilized Government. Examining the country in the light which I have had the honour to bring before your Lordship, it will be conceived that nothing but narrow-minded prejudice or low servility to principles and policies of government already exploded since the conclusion of the ill-fated Ashantee war can induce any one to hamper any legitimate, loyal, and democratic measures tending to improve the tribes in the interior.

I do not believe, my Lord, that any European Government can effect this improved state of things in the interior without an enormous outlay, and we natives of the Coast believe your Lordship per-

sonally, and the Government of Her Majesty the
Queen, whose Secretary of the Colonies you are,
hail with delight any loyal, legitimate, and approved
means employed by the natives of the Coast to
further any political improvement amongst their
countrymen, so as not only to relieve the Imperial
exchequer from its heavy outlay, but also to lessen
the awful responsibility of the Home Government
on matters relating to so distant and unhealthy a
colony. That means, in the interior of the Gold
Coast, is the formation of a Confederation of all
their kings, recognizing one person of influence as
their superior, and organizing a constitutional Government, loyal to the British sea-coast Government.

The Fantee Confederation, as I have stated in
my Letter No. II., sprung into existence soon after
the exchange of territory between the English and
Dutch Governments, and its main object is to
advance the interests of the whole of the Fantee
nation, and to combine for offence and defence in
time of war ; the tentative manner in which it has
been carried on for nearly two years, and the
influence and power which it had over the kings in
the interior, especially when not hampered by petty

annoyances from the sea-coast Government, is a sufficient guarantee that it is the most needful and necessary constitution to advance the civilization of the interior tribes, which, if left dependent on the narrow and limited Government of the sea-coast, will remain in utter barbarism. It is, therefore, the anxious wish of every civilized native of the Gold Coast, who has the interest of his country at heart, that in this agitated political state of the interior, a great desideratum to their country would be to get a *Codex Constitutionum* from the British Government on the sea-coast, defining their powers, giving them extensive latitude to improve the interior, without their President, or whatever the head of the Government might be called, being subjected to constant humiliation by being ordered up to Cape Coast ; in fact, so as to give " stability, distinctness, and extent to principles before unsettled, indefinite, and limited in their operations ;" such laws as would form the basis of further political devevelopment.

The Fantee Confederation is necessary to be established as a compact Government of the Fantee race :—

First. Because in a dispatch from the Right Hon. Edward Cardwell, when Secretary of State for the Colonies, to the Government of Cape Coast in 1864, after the disastrous and ill-fated Ashantee expedition, the kings were ordered to be told that they were *not to receive protection* in future from the British Government. Lieutenant-Governor Conran, in a despatch to the Secretary of State for the Colonies, dated 7th October, 1865, informed him that he had put up a notice defining the limits of British territory to a distance of a cannon shot or five miles from each castle or fort, so as to bring the natives within our laws, and check lawlessness amongst them, but not interfering with domestic slavery. Mr. Cardwell, in a reply dated November, 1865, distinctly informed him that he was " unable to approve the step which he," Colonel Conran, " had taken in declaring the territory within five miles of eight separate British forts to be British territory," and requested him to " recall the notice in which he had done it ;" and in a subsequent despatch, dated December 22nd, 1865, he expressly told him to " avoid any expression," in any notice issued by him, " which bore the appearance of extended jurisdiction over territory at the Gold Coast."

Second. Because the Confederation will in no

way interfere with the British authority on the sea-coast, but will aid greatly in putting down cruel punishments and exactions which are practised by native interior chiefs.

Third. Because it will form a compact governing body, composed of men of intelligence, protecting the boundary line on the frontier of Ashantee, their implacable enemy, and capable of exhibiting such force as would resist any attempt at invasion.

Fourth. Because the Coast Government has done nothing, nor is it likely to do anything in years to come, towards the improvement of the interior towns.

Fifth. Because in all previous invasions of the Fantee territory, the Ashantee forces, since the battle of Doodoowah in 1822, have cunningly avoided the sea-coast towns where British troops are stationed, but have ravaged the interior towns ; and there being no compact governing body, and no superior leader, the Ashantee forces have succeeded in destroying each province in detail.

Sixth. Because the Dutch Government is an ally of the constant enemy of the Fantees—the Ashantees; and the exchange of territory, if accepted by the Wassaws and Denkeras in the interior of the Dutch sea-coast towns, will open a high road immediately for the Ashantees, which would give them considerable power over the Fantee nation, and would lead to constant trouble on the sea-coast. That the Wassaws and Denkeras, who had thrown off the yoke of Ashantee for the flag of England, having refused to accept the Dutch flag, and having made overtures to the Fantee nation, who are composed of innumerable kings governing various provinces, to form an alliance with it, it was absolutely necessary that there should be a central Government, from which there should proceed the wishes of the nation from recognized and approved authority.

Seventh. Because the Coast Government declines giving sufficient and adequate protection to those who might attempt to develop the mineral resources of the country, by placing officers of the peace in the districts or provinces where the diggings are worked, so as to prevent the chiefs from molesting them, as the chiefs in the interior exhibit very little respect towards the interference of the Government on the coast in their social arrangements, unless the Governor is able to march troops into their provinces and compel the execution of his orders.

Eighth.—Because wars have broken out in the interior towns in the neighbourhood of the towns on the sea-coast; the country has been invaded by hostile tribes; treaties signed and sealed by these hostile tribes with the British authority have been broken; and no physical force was sent by the Governor (nor by orders can he do so) to quell the disturbance, but guns and ammunition were given to the natives, who were left to do the best they could to repel the invaders.

Ninth. Because education and industrial pursuits have never been encouraged by the authorities on the Coast amongst the interior tribes, and there is no reason to believe that they will ever be encouraged. Consequently it requires the interior tribes to organize a body of men who will give the subject that attention and consideration which it deserves, without, however, interfering with the Coast authorities.

Tenth. Because the Gold Coast is considered by the Home authorities as an expensive Protectorate, the authority of the British Government is limited to a very great extent to the sea-coast towns, and the people still maintain their time-honoured customs and practices, which, although in direct opposition and repugnant to the British Colonial Constitution, are tolerated and allowed free latitude. That in the interior the Coast Government cannot put down the more abominable practices; and a native Government, whose authority is recognized and accepted by all the kings, will have a great deal more power to put them down.

These are, my Lord, the reasons which I am able to discover, and which, if carefully considered by an unprejudiced mind, will be regarded as sufficient inducement to give the Fantee Confederation all the support requisite for its compact formation.

Since the formation of the present Confederation the whole of the Fantee nation has been combined under one Government, whose status, although ill-defined, carries great weight and influence amongst the interior tribes. It forms a representative body, to whom the various tribes who are anxious to become allies of the Fantee race have been able to communicate their wishes. It is the pivot of national unity, headed by intelligent men, to whom a great· deal of the powers of the kings and chiefs are delegated, and whose advice would have considerable weight and power. Through it the whole of the Fantee race, numbering some 400,000 souls,

can now, for the first time, boast of a national
assembly, in which have congregated not only
various kings and chiefs in scattered provinces, far
and wide, but also the intelligence of Fantee-
land.   It makes the King of Ashantee for the first
time throw off his supercilious disregard of the
formerly disunited Fantee race, and tremble for
the safety of his kingdom.   When the Confederate
tribes menaced it with the weight and power of their
combined army, even the King of Ashantee felt
the influence of the Confederation, and sent conciliatory messages to its Court at Mankessim.   It
enables the whole of the Fantee race to possess a
national purse, by which it is enabled in time of war
to supply each province with means for the purchase
of war materials, and also to send material aid to its
allies in men and money.   The utility of the Confederation to the interior tribes is undoubted, and
its power and influence are increased in arithmetical
progression according to the support and countenance it receives from the Governor or Administrator
on the sea-coast.   When it is befriended ·by the
Governor, when he lends it his advice and counsel,
when he supports its legitimate measures, and does
not regard it with a jealous eye, the Confederation

grows strong for good, its officers receive great respect, the kings and chiefs have great confidence in it, and its commands are greatly respected. But when the Governor or Administrator circumvents the officers of the Confederation with petty annoyances, and humiliates its President in every possible way before the eyes of the nation, the interest of the Confederation, and the good results which its formation prognosticated, become checked ; and the Coast Government, which at present does not attempt to develop the interior provinces, retards rather than supports its organization.

It is on this ground that there is now a loud cry for a *codex constitutionum* for the Confederation from the Government of the Coast. It is essential so that every branch of the Government should have its power and limits well defined, protecting it against aggression, and " ascertaining the purposes for which the Government exists," and the rights which are guaranteed to it ; securing its rights in the various provinces, and restraining it from exercising functions which would endanger liberty and justice. The present drooping state of the Confederation can say with great truth, *novus rerum nascitur ordo*— a new order of things is generated.

There are, no doubt, many intelligent natives on the sea-coast who are well disposed towards the Confederation. Some of these men have told me that, on account of the undefined and unstable state of the Confederation, they have been afraid to act their part towards it according to their feelings and influences, which they would immediately do were the British Government on the Coast to countenance and support it in such a manner as to lead them to believe that it would not, on slight occasions, use its power to embarrass and ultimately suppress it.

In a pamphlet on the political economy of British Western Africa, with the requirements of the several colonies and settlements, published by me in 1865, I remarked in paragraph 1, page 6, that "it will be necessary for the Government to be very circumspect in the selection of its officials for the Coast, and that the Governor-General, in particular, should be a man who possesses a happy tact and natural sagacity combined with experience, so as to hit the right course, since to him will be given the ground-plan of the future political government. He should make it his first object to discover those salutary measures which are necessary, and endeavour to counteract those noxious influences which may sap the healthy action of the community. He must make himself perfectly acquainted with the internal affairs of each colony, its revenues and expenses, its commerce and agriculture, with the national character of the inhabitants, and each section of their Government. He should form a correct judgment of the character of every prominent official in his Government, and he should possess a talent for comprehensive and rapid observations in the selection of fit instruments for different appointments." I am happy to say, my Lord, that the present Governor-in-Chief of the West African Settlements, Sir Arthur Kennedy, is one who has fulfilled the hopes of the general public—one who answers to the general description of the high official necessary for the whole Coast. He is the right man in the right place, and to him must the people on the Gold Coast look as the steersman at the helm of the Fantee national vessel to guide it safely into a quiet and peaceful haven.*

The Constitution between the English Government on the sea-coast and the Fantee Confederation

---

* The following memorial portrays in an especial manner the feeling of the public in Western Africa :—

should be somewhat distinct from that of the Act of Confederation between the kings themselves; but this latter Act should be supervised and modelled according to the position of the different kings and their provinces, as well as the condition of the people, by the administrative power on the Coast, by which means it will carry a far greater degree of

---

"*To his Excellency Sir A. E. Kennedy, C.B., Governor-in-Chief of the West African Settlements.*

"FREETOWN, *Nov.*, 1869.

"MAY IT PLEASE YOUR EXCELLENCY,

"The Memorial of the Sierra Leone native pastors in connexion with the Church of England, under the auspices of the venerable Church Missionary Society, humbly and respectfully sheweth :—

"That your memorialists hail with unmingled pleasure and satisfaction the recent appointment of the Rev. George Nicol, late pastor of St. Charles, Regent, to the vacant chaplaincy of the Gambia, as an era in the history of the West African settlements; and that, whilst your memorialists thus give expression to their feelings for the honour conferred on one of their body, they cannot let pass this opportunity without expressing with thankfulness to your Excellency their firm conviction that to the influence of your high position is due the credit of this appointment.

"Your memorialists will ever regard with unfeigned gratitude to Almighty God the consecration of the Rev. Dr. Crowther to the bishopric of the Niger territory, as a crowning act of British Christian philanthropy; the admission of Drs. Horton and Davies as staff assistant-surgeons in the service of Her Most Gracious Majesty as a proof of British goodwill for the sons of Africa; but they regard the present appointment with a lively interest as peculiar

power, weight, and influence amongst the kings themselves. The position and jurisdiction of the British authority and the Fantee Confederation must be strictly defined and definitely laid down, the position of the Administration of the Gold Coast to the Confederation properly regulated, and the sources of revenue, whether by a grant from the

---

in its character, in that whilst Dr. Crowther is a missionary bishop, exercising the functions of his office in a territory not under British rule, and Drs. Davies and Horton are employed in an entirely military capacity, this is a civil ecclesiastical appointment to a post not hitherto known in the history of these settlements to have been filled by any in a full capacity except by Europeans.

" Your memorialists regard the appointment in question as an earnest of a happier day for the West African settlements, when the prejudices of race, so prevalent in countries where civilization, literature, and refinement in manners are in the growth, will be at an end. They need hardly say that to you, dear Sir Arthur, they look with eager expectations for the speedy fulfilment of this blessed time, for in this appointment, as in others of inferior though not of small importance otherwise, you have shown a just appreciation of merit and character, and not a regard to mere accident.

" Your memorialists cannot conclude without assuring your Excellency of their affectionate goodwill towards you personally, and recording their gratitude to Earl Granville (to whom may it please your Excellency to convey these expressions of our feelings) and the British Government, and to the venerable Church Missionary Society, to whose untiring and praiseworthy efforts three-fourths of the educated portion in this colony are indebted.

" God save the Queen !

(Signed)   " THE NATIVE PASTORS."

custom dues or by a small export duty on produce, considered. Ample provision should be made for the education of the young in every province, either by the employment of teachers by the officers of the Confederation, or by subsidizing the Wesleyans for that express purpose. A distinct plan should be laid down for the purpose of improving the industry of the interior tribes, and for developing the mineral resources.

The object of the Confederation being not only for social improvement, but also to secure external as well as internal peace, the Administrator of the Gold Coast should be *ex officio*, by the Act of Confederation, the *Protector of the Fantee Confederation*. There should then be elected a president, two ministers—viz., one who superintends internal and external affairs, and the other industry and education—and a chief justice. For the purpose of deliberating on the mutual affairs of the Confederate states, a Confederate Diet should be established at Mankessim, having two divisions—the Royal, in which all the kings, with the principal chiefs or grandees, should have seats ; the other, the Representative Assembly, to which each province should send a certain number of representatives, obtained by the votes of all the citizens. The fundamental law of the country should guarantee to every citizen equal rights and protection, and direct or indirect participation in the Government. These Assemblies should have the power of legislating for the Confederate provinces, the right of declaring peace or war (when the interest of the Government of the Coast is not concerned), of forming alliances, of regulating the taxation, the police, industrial pursuits, education, &c. Disputes of the Confederate provinces to be decided at the Royal Diet, and the decision open to appeal to the Governor. The President of the Confederation should be made, *ex officio*, a member of the Legislative Council, where his presence should only be required when subjects affecting or relating to the interest of the Confederation are about to be discussed ; and should he hold that appointment as a Government nominee prior to his election, he should be called upon to resign it as such, but assume the position of membership as President of the Confederation.

Ce n'est que le premier pas qui coute.

I have the honour to be, my Lord,

Your Lordship's most obedient Servant,

J. A. B. HORTON, M.D.

APPENDIX.

No. I.

STATEMENTS OF MR. FYNN.

I was at Dixcove when the change of flags took place, and afterwards was removed by the Mission to " Secondee." I saw an Accra man named Apainin, who was attempting to reach Cape Coast, killed by the Dutch " Secondees." I saw his head and tongue, which had been cut off, lying on the ground; I also saw his body, and was much frightened, and determined to go away to Cape Coast. Mr. Leighton, some time after, came up in a vessel to " Secondee," and I applied to him for a passage for my wife and family to Cape Coast, which he granted. The kings of Secondee, on my telling them this, were opposed to my departure, as they and their children would be deprived of my services. They would not allow me to go, and recommended me to the protection of the Commandant, named Van Drap, who was kind, and interested himself for me. Governor Nagtglas came up shortly after in the man-of-war " Kroopman." He asked me if I would like to go to Cape Coast or remain. I said I had now no reason to go. He therefore told me I was free to stop and follow my affairs. The king and people wished me to stay.

Wishing to send my wife and people to Cape Coast, however, I asked for a passage for them on board a vessel, which was granted. But when I got my family to the beach, the king and all the people went to the Commandant and told him they could not allow my family to go; that the Ashantees were coming, and that I must wait until they passed to Elmina.

When the master of the vessel heard this, he also refused to embark my people. The Commandant then advised me to come to the fort for safety, which I did not do. He said, "Well, send your family, and I will send two soldiers to protect you from Atjiempon" (the Ashantee headman). The Ashantees arrived and went into the fort, and sent for me. The Commandant told them who I was, and that I was there by desire of Governor Nagtglas. Then Atjiempon blamed the Governor for allowing me to be there, and referred to the capture by the Commendahs of the Dutch sailors, and the treatment of Elminas by Fantees. He also said the Governor did it because he feared the English, and he then returned in angry state to the town.

It happened that seven Fantees were detained in the fort, having been taken by the Secondees, and these men were demanded by the Ashantees for the purpose of being killed.

The Commandant gave up six men to the Ashantees. I and my family were then staying in the fort, as the Commandant feared the Ashantees would kill me. The Secondees then came and demanded I should be delivered up, but the Commandant would not.

When the six Fantees were delivered up, they were handed to the Ashantees by the Secondees, and put in irons.

The Secondees made a desperate attempt to force the gates to get me, but could not. Atjiempon then announced his intention of getting me out himself, to kill me; on which the Commandant wrote to Colonel Nagtglas, who told Atjiempon to do no harm to the Fantees. The Commandant wrote again to the Governor. The Ashantees made light of the Governor's orders, and said they would kill me. In the evening, as my property was being transported from the mission-house to the fort, a portion was plundered by the Secondees. Next morning the man-of-war "Amstel" came. The Commandant sent for Atjiempon and sent him off, and I was taken on board with my family. I thought I was going to Cape Coast; but, alas! they let go anchor at Commendah, and gave me to another man-of-war, the "Kroopman." The captain of her told me I was now a Dutchman, and that I would remain and meet the Ashantees. Three days after his Excellency the Governor came up, and told me that I must remain in the man-of-war, to meet the Ashantees at Commendah, as he had something against them; and also because Atjiempon (the Ashantee) had made the Governor's head officer swear that I should not be allowed to go to Cape Coast till they came to Elmina and got 300oz. from Colonel Nagtglas. For these reasons I was to remain. After the arrival of the Ashantees I was to go to Cape Coast. Three days after, the commander of the "Kroopman" imprisoned me in the third story down below from the evening to the morning, because I spoke to some Elmina canoemen. He determined therefore to put me in irons. I went on board on the 5th December, and arrived at Cape Coast on the 27th. During this time I could for three days scarcely obtain water and food. I wrote to the Governor for permission to come ashore, but received no answer.

With regard to the six men (Fantees) delivered to the Ashantees at Secondee, I have always heard that they were killed, as well as a poor old Fantee man named Reynolds. His Excellency promised that he would get back all my property from Secondee.

I should be ungrateful not to speak well of Governor Nagtglas's kindness to me.

I do solemnly and sincerely declare that the foregoing statement is correct and true in every particular.

(Signed)   JOSIAH A. FYNN,
A Schoolmaster.

Declared before me this 6th day of January, 1870.

THOMAS JONES, J.P.

No. II.

AFFIDAVIT OF MR. WILLIAM EDWARD SAM.

Personally appeared before me, Charles B. Mosse, Esquire, one of Her Majesty's Justices of the Peace for the Settlements on the Gold Coast of Africa, one William Edward Sam, who being duly sworn, saith as follows:—

I was born at a village on the seaboard adjoining Cape Coast, called Amamful, and believe I am about thirty-two years of age. I have always considered myself a British subject. I am in the employ of Messrs. F. and A. Swanzy, of London and West Africa, and have held a responsible position in the service of that firm over four, and nearly five, years, and believe I have always given satisfaction.

For some time previous to the fifteenth day of last month I have had charge of a factory or establishment belonging to the aforesaid firm of F. and A. Swanzy at the town of Dixcove, that town having been ceded to the Dutch Government by the British Government in the month of January of last year.

On Saturday, the 12th day of June, 1869, P. W. Alvarez, Commandant of the said town of Dixcove, went round the town with armed soldiers to take an account of gunpowder in all the merchants' stores, placing a guard upon every house supposed to contain that article. The last house he went to was Mr. Quabina Mensah's, in the magazine of which was stored a large quantity of gunpowder. Shortly after the Commandant left me, at Messrs. Swanzy's factory, I heard the report of a rifle in the direction the Commandant had taken. I was informed that the Commandant had ordered the removal of Mr. Mensah's gunpowder to the fort, without giving any explanation beyond saying that he was acting on the Governor's instructions, and, on that account, Mr. Mensah had objected. There appeared to be great excitement; and I was further informed that the rifle was fired by one of the soldiers as a signal for re-inforcements from the fort. Shortly after this more armed soldiers arrived from the fort. On my interposition it was agreed by both parties that the store containing the gunpowder should be sealed with the Government seal. The Commandant then went back to the fort for seal and wax. He returned; but refused to put a seal upon the door of the magazine, saying that he had been told that some of the gunpowder had been removed during his absence, and that, therefore, he must remove it all to the fort.

Mr. Mensah still refused to allow his gunpowder to be removed; and while he and the Commandant were in the upper part of the house, the soldiers removed from the lower part three chests, each containing twenty guns, that were under cover outside the stores; and this was so quietly done (no reference having been made to the removal of guns) that Mr. Mensah was not aware of the robbery until they were half way to the fort. On the Commandant's return to the fort he sent a soldier to tell all the Elmina people residing in Dixcove to go to the fort on hearing the report of a cannon. The soldier came to Messrs. Swanzy's factory twice to tell some Elmina people in their employ to go to the fort when they heard the cannon; and these people said they would not go. About half an hour after this a cannon fired, and all the Elmina people rushed into the fort, except those in the factory of my employers, carrying their personal effects with them. Seeing this, I felt greatly concerned for the safety of the property in my charge, and instantly wrote to the Commandant to the following effect: "I am quite alarmed at the signal of guns and rush of Elmina people into the fort. What is the matter? and what am I to do with Messrs. F. and A. Swanzy's property in case of any disturbance in the town? Pray, Sir, put me in the way, and I will endeavour to prevent any such thing." Shortly afterwards the Commandant came to the factory and informed me that the signal from the fort was merely intended to collect the Elmina people together to assist in conveying Mr. Mensah's gunpowder to the fort, as he, the Commandant, was determined to have the gunpowder on that day; at the same time he gave me to understand that I need have no apprehension concerning the safety of the property under my charge. He returned to the fort, and shortly afterwards marched with ten or eleven of his soldiers to take Mr. Mensah a prisoner. Mr. Mensah's people seeing this prepared to resist the Commandant. When the Commandant reached the gate of Messrs. Swanzy's factory I ran down and begged hard that he would not make such a perilous attempt, pointing out to him the danger of it. The soldiers, seeing the folly of what was about to take place, urged me to dissuade the Commandant from proceeding further, and I prevailed on him to return to the fort. At the same time he sent me, in company with one of the Government landing waiters, to tell Mr. Mensah that if he did not deliver up his gunpowder that day he would ask the interference of the Bushwah people to compel him to do so. Bushwah is the name of a place near Dixcove, and the chief of all the Ahanta towns. Mr. Mensah still refused to deliver his gunpowder, and, to prevent bloodshed and destruction of property in the town through the interference of the Bushwah people in the matter, I went back to the fort, and offered one hundred ounces of gold dust as security, in the name of Messrs. Swanzy, that Mr. Mensah's gunpowder should not be sold or used in the event of making custom, or even of war, without the authority of the Commandant, or, in his absence, anyone representing the Dutch Government, the Government seals being first placed on the magazine. The Commandant thanked me for this offer, but expressed his regret that he could not accept it, on the ground that it would appear he had not carried out his instructions. I now found that danger was greatly to be apprehended, and that my entreaties and suggestions were of no avail to prevent it. At last I proposed to the Commandant that, instead of going further into the matter that day, the best plan would be to let it stand over, and to write to the Governor of Elmina for further instructions, and meanwhile to give Mr. Mensah and the chiefs an opportunity to communicate in writing to the Governor their reasons for refusing to give up their gunpowder to the Commandant. The Commandant consented to this arrangement, and sent me immediately to Mr. Mensah and the chiefs to inform them of it, and request them to send some one with the landing waiter to the fort to represent them. Letters were immediately written by the Com-

mandant, Mr. Mensah, and the two chiefs of the town, addressed
to the Governor of Elmina. Mr. Mensah's and the chiefs' letters
were afterwards taken by me into the fort for the Commandant's in-
spection, who countersigned them after having read them, and they
were dispatched with one from him to Elmina. I wrote a brief note,
with the Commandant's permission, in the fort to the agent of
Messrs. F. and A. Swanzy, Mr. W. Cleaver, to the following
effect : " I write this in the fort. There is a hard palaver between
the Government and Mr. Mensah for refusing to give up his gunpowder to be lodged in the fort. I have tried to prevent bloodshed
to-day. The Commandant has written for a man-of-war. Try and
come up in her, as you have more influence with Mr. Mensah than
anyone else representing Messrs. Swanzy." This was also signed
and approved by the Commandant. The canoe was dispatched
about 5 P.M. On Sunday morning, the 13th of June, the Elmina
people being still in the fort, and afraid to enter the town to buy
food, I consulted Mr. Mensah and the two chiefs in reference to the
propriety of sending the gong-gong round the town to caution the
people against molesting the Elminas, and to direct them to sell
provisions to the Elmina people ; and this was done. I accompanied the crier with the gong-gong, and it was beaten outside the
fort as well as the town. After this I went to the Commandant
and reported the fact. Towards the afternoon the sergeant came to
the factory and complained that he had been abused by some of
Mr. Mensah's people, and said that if I were to let the Commandant alone in this matter the town would be destroyed instantaneously.
I begged his pardon, and told him not to mention anything to the
Commandant, and gave him about twenty pounds of rice for himself
and men. He seemed satisfied, and went back to the fort. This
was all that happened that morning.

About seven o'clock in the evening of the same day, I heard that
Dixcove was surrounded by Ahanta people. I forthwith went to
the forts and asked the Commandant if the report was true. He
said, " Yes ;" but that he could not prevent the people coming,
because Mr. Mensah and his boy Brahoon would not go to the fort
as prisoners for refusing to give up the gunpowder. I was rather

astonished, as nothing had occurred on the part of the Dixcove people to give annoyance to the Commandant since the letters were dispatched to Elmina; and I offered fifty ounces of gold dust as security for the good conduct of Mr. Mensah and Brahoon until an answer should come from the Governor. The Commandant refused this offer on the ground that the enemy were so near that he could not stop them. I then begged him to allow me to send to Quaw Eshon, the paramount chief of Ahanta, and his chiefs one puncheon of rum and ten large cases of gin to stop their people from attacking Dixcove until an answer should come from Elmina, telling him meantime of my friendship with the aforesaid Quaw Eshon, through which I had no doubt I could effect the desired objects; but he would not allow me to carry out my proposal. This was repeated over and over again, but all to no purpose. He only said he thought it proper to give the Rev. T. Laing and myself notice in writing in the morning to remove our property to the fort, which notice he failed to give.

It was now nearly midnight; and I went to the town greatly distressed.

On my arrival at the entrance of the factory I met three men, caught by Dixcove people, who were taken as spies from Bushwah, and, as they were about to be ill-treated, I tried to rescue them by waiting upon the two chiefs or kings, who at once took them from the people, and gave them to me to be delivered to the Commandant for safety, as they had no palaver with the Government. I took them to the Commandant the same night, and while in the fort I recognized the guns stolen from Mr. Mensah's house in possession of the Elmina people.

At this time I had no hopes of doing anything to prevent bloodshed and destruction of property. I returned to the factory with the goldtaker, and, while meditating what other methods to adopt, I suddenly heard a knock at the factory gate. On its being opened, one of the Government landing waiters, with two armed soldiers, came in, the former with a letter in his hand, which, he said, was addressed to the Governor of Elmina; and he told me that the Commandant sent him and the two soldiers expressly to inform me that he had considered all my troubles and endeavours to prevent bloodshed, and found it expedient to take my advice, and wait until an answer should come from Elmina, and for that purpose they had been sent to Bushwah to tell King Quaw Eshon and his people that if they attacked Dixcove before the answer came from Elmina, the responsibility would rest with him (Quaw Eshon) and not with the Dutch Government. It cannot be easily imagined how glad I was to hear this news; and I immediately took the three messengers to the two chiefs of Dixcove, who were also very glad to hear the news, and gave four armed men to escort the Commandant's messengers half way to Bushwah. I accompanied these people, and returned to Dixcove, intending to return shortly to meet them at about the same place, and did so.

The Government messengers returned at about 5.30 on Monday morning with news that all was settled. I accompanied them to the fort gate, and returned to the factory, having been up all night. At about six o'clock, the Commandant went round the town with soldiers. He came to the factory in company with a chief called Ahimadakis, and the Commandant told the chief and myself, in the presence of several witnesses, that all was settled, and that he wanted to see Mr. Mensah and both chiefs in the fort at eleven o'clock. The Commandant took a glass of wine with me, and then returned to the fort.

It is really painful as well as astonishing to find that, notwithstanding the assurances of the Commandant that all was settled, that, in about a quarter of an hour from the time that he left the factory to go to the fort, Dixcove was attacked on every side by an army of Bushwahs. The Commandant then came to the factory with three soldiers. I inquired what the matter was, and he replied, " An attack from Bushwah," when I began to blame him for deceiving me, telling him that he was perfectly aware that my life and the property were not safe from either side in case of a fight between the people of Bushwah and Dixcove. He then declared before the Rev. Mr. Laing and myself that the Bushwah people were acting in direct opposition to his orders, given not more than two hours before. Mr. Laing then said to him, " If the people are acting contrary to your orders, it is then your duty to defend Dixcove against them." "That I will not do," the Commandant replied. I then told him to come with me to the field to endeavour to persuade the attacking party to retire. He refused to do so. Then I offered him the keys of the factory, as I considered the property in great danger. He refused at first; but after some expostulations he promised to accompany me to the field where the forces were collected, when his soldiers refused to go, and, as he could not compel them, he marched back to the fort. I then went alone to the field, and desired the Dixcove people not to fire upon the attacking party, as the Commandant was coming to send back the Bushwah people; and I requested the Rev. Mr. Laing to go to the fort to beg the Commandant to come out. Mr. Laing went to the fort, and returned, informing me that the gates of the fort were closed, that the Commandant was on the ramparts, and that, seeing Mr. Laing, he told him he could not be admitted, but that if he had anything to say he would hear him as they were situated. Mr. Laing then begged the Commandant to go to the field to send back the attacking party. He said he would not go.

A few minutes after this, I heard firing at one end of the field. I ran to the spot with my hat in my hand, shouting as loud as I could to the attacking forces, "Pardon, pardon! fifty ounces of gold " dust for satisfaction." They kept rushing forward notwithstanding; and I narrowly escaped with my life. I saw a good many Dutch native soldiers with their Snider rifles, who killed many of the Dixcove people. The fighting, with slight intermission, lasted all day; and the enemy were repulsed on every occasion. Between ten and eleven o'clock Mr. Laing sent to tell me that our factory had been fired at by cannon from the fort, and that a part of the premises had been destroyed thereby; and I heard the firing of heavy ordnance all day.

As Mr. Alvarez had both publicly and privately told me the Elmina people residing in Dixcove, then living in the fort, had rancorous feelings against me, and as he seemed to be much under their influence, I concluded at once by this unprovoked attack of his upon Messrs. F. and A. Swanzy's factory, he would by some indirect means injure my life during the fight. I therefore resolved to remain in the field, in order to avoid that danger, and that I might escape to the bush should the enemy overcome us. At the close of the day, when the enemy had retired, and some of the Dixcove people were about returning to the town, they were fired upon from the fort with rifles and heavy ordnance, and were therefore obliged to retire into the bush; and I accompanied them.

I returned to Dixcove after seven or eight days, when I heard that the Bushwah people, after burning or otherwise destroying the town, had left the place. I found the store walls of Messrs. Swanzy's factory knocked down, part of the roof off, and the whole of the property removed or destroyed, excepting sixty puncheon packs, which have been since removed by me with the consent of the officer in charge of the fort. Scales for weighing gold and my private writing desk were shown me by the Commandant inside the fort, and I accepted the latter. The property consisted of a large quantity of cotton goods—both loose and in original packages— rum, tobacco, and other merchandize, about ninety-seven puncheons of palm oil, a large quantity of palm kernels, gold dust, cash, &c. The safe containing cash and gold dust had been removed, and all the books and accounts of the establishment.

In conversation with Mr. Alvarez after my return to Dixcove, he acknowledged that a large quantity of Messrs. F. and A. Swanzy's property had been taken into the fort by the soldiers and Elmina people, but had since been removed. He said he knew at the time the goods were being removed, but had not the power to prevent it. He expected the Dutch man-of-war to arrive at Dixcove shortly, and he intended on her arrival to take the property from the native soldiers by the aid of the marines, but when the man-of-war arrived the goods were all gone. Speaking of the burning of the town, the Commandant said he had been asked by the Elmina people in the fort to allow them to go out and set fire to the town during the fight, but he would not permit it; but that shortly after, being tired, he went to bed, and when he awoke he found the town was in flames. I found the iron safe belonging to the factory broken to pieces, close to the walls of the fort. I called the Commandant's attention to it; he laughed, and did not appear at all surprised. I have no doubt the safe was stolen and broken up by the Dutch native soldiers. I saw a quantity of Messrs. Swanzy's goods in charge of the soldiers in the fort, which I heard and believe they were selling at about half their value. I bought two flasks of gin, the label and stamp of which was like what I had in the factory, of one of the soldiers inside the fort.

One day, while inside the said fort, a soldier on guard called me aside and offered to show me where he had seen some of his comrades hide a puncheon of palm oil, belonging to Messrs. Swanzy, if I would make him a present. I refused to have anything to do with him.

It is seriously believed that the Dutch Government brought about the destruction of Dixcove, preparations having been previously made for the event, as three days before the commencement of the palaver—that is, Wednesday, the 9th day of June—munitions of war were sent from Elmina to all the kings and chiefs of all the towns surrounding Dixcove, excepting only the Dixcove people, and the town was simultaneously attacked from places to windward as well as leeward.

(Signed)   W. E. SAM.

Sworn before me this 20th day of July, 1869, at Cape Coast Castle.

(Signed)   C. B. MOSSE, J.P.